YORKSHIRE MINING VETERANS

DEDICATION

In memory of:

Frank Beverley
Mick Carter
John Willie Clamp
Arthur Clayton
Bernard Goddard
Tommy Henwood
Fred Hiscock
Stanley Potter
Dennis Rodgers
Jack Steer
Harry Taylor

who contributed so much to this book but
passed away before its publication.

Frank Beverley, 1923–2005
*Ex Dodworth, Darfield Main, Woolley,
Haigh, Wharncliffe Woodmoor 4&5,
Redbrook and Rob Royd Collieries*

Yorkshire Mining Veterans
In Their Own Words

MINING HERITAGE
SERIES

Compiled and Edited by
Brian Elliott

Volume I

Wharncliffe Books

First Published in Great Britain in 2005 by
Wharncliffe Books
an imprint of
Pen and Sword Books Ltd.
47 Church Street
Barnsley
South Yorkshire
S70 2AS

Copyright © Brian Elliott 2005

ISBN: 1-903425-58-1

Typeset in 10/12pt Century Old Style by Mac Style Ltd, Scarborough.

Printed and bound in England by
CPI UK.

Pen and Sword Books Ltd incorporates the Imprints of
Pen & Sword Aviation, Pen & Sword Maritime,
Pen & Sword Military, Wharncliffe Books,
Pen & Sword Select, Pen and Sword Military Classics
and Leo Cooper.

For a complete list of Pen & Sword titles please contact
PEN & SWORD BOOKS LIMITED
47 Church Street
Barnsley
South Yorkshire
S70 2BR
England
E-mail: enquiries@pen-and-sword.co.uk
Website: www.pen-and-sword.co.uk

Contents

Harry Taylor (1913–2005)
Ex Rob Royd, Dodworth
(Church Lane) & Monk
Bretton Collieries

Foreword

A book like *Yorkshire Mining Veterans* is long overdue since it catalogues the stories of miners and their very real experiences of working in coal-mines. Here we have not only accounts of comradeship but of hardship and struggle.

This book is a social history of mining in the twentieth century and one to which anyone can relate, especially those who worked in the industry and experienced the sudden shock of that first day at work.

I hope that those who have not been miners who read Brian Elliott's book will gain an understanding of why we, as miners, are who we are, what makes us forever members of a special fraternity and why our hearts sink whenever we hear about mining disasters anywhere in the world.

For those who have worked in the industry Brian's book will bring all the memories of working underground and on the pit-top back to life, told by miners themselves. Nothing could be more authentic.

Brian Elliott has done a service to working class people and to social history, in fact anyone reading his compilation will be able to capture for themselves the unique experience that is coalmining.

Steve Kemp
National Secretary, National Union of Mineworkers
Barnsley, May 2005

Introduction

More than thirty years ago John Burnett compiled a marvellous collection of first-hand experiences of working people based on previously unpublished autobiographies and diaries.[1] His collection included extracts from the writings of two coalminers: Thomas Jordan (b.1892), a Durham hewer who hated pit-work and B L Coombes (b.1894), a collier who was one of the first to use a mechanical coal-cutter in South Wales. Also included were the memories of Emmanuel Lovekin (b.1820) who worked as a door-trapper,[2] in a south Staffordshire pit at the age of just seven and a half and, surviving several accidents, to became a 'butty-man'[3] He went on to obtain a colliery manager's certificate. Throughout his life Lovekin was a Primitive Methodist and worked as a Sunday School teacher. His life story is a classic tale of self-education, hard-graft and religious faith for modest financial return.

There are echoes, enhancements and extensions of Jordan, Coombes and Lovekin in my collection of mining memories, some of them reaching back to at least the early nineteenth century: Stan Potter (b.1922), tramming with a candle for light; Ernest Kaye (b.1917) working in the dark as a lonely door-trapper; Tommy Henwood (b.1912), stubbornly labouring naked alongside his father – despite the visit of the Mayor's lady; and Eric Crabtree's (b. 1932) eerie visit into the old Cadeby workings where the terrible 1912 disaster had taken place. Religion and self-education are certainly prominent in testimonies and achievements of several older veterans: local historian Arthur Clayton (b.1901) whose scholarly research, writing and teaching has inspired and educated so many people; Gerald Booth's (b.1909) sensitive musical compositions and his outstanding record as a Methodist preacher, a role also evidently important for George Rawson (b.1913) whose autobiographical writings are always well-received.

For many miners the transition to deputy status via study and qualifications did not appeal but others gained their 'ticket' and their comments about this rôle make interesting reading. A few former boy miners gained promotion through the ranks to management status. Ted Lunness, for example, managed Cortonwood and Manvers and became a consultant. The remarkable career of Bernard Goddard spanned well over sixty years, including a notable spell as the youngest HM Inspector of Mines, before returning to the grassroots of mine management; and later to international consultancy.

One of the most remarkable characteristics in many of my interviews, particularly with the older men, was the uncomplaining acceptance of past conditions of life and work which, to modern readers and listeners, seem brutal, degrading, even unimaginable. The long term effects of working in dusty conditions have become well-known in recent years through the huge number of compensation claims relating to respiratory diseases. The situation was brought home to me in my interview with George Kemp (b.1920) who spoke with such courage, despite his ever-present breathing problems.

The clearest recollections were those relating to leaving school and starting work. The amount of detail that could be remembered, sixty, seventy or even ninety years later was truly astounding.

Poverty was widespread in Yorkshire mining communities during the early years of the twentieth century but that did stop miners and their families supporting their Union's efforts to campaign for better pay and conditions. Childhood and even adult memories of the 1926 strike are still evident in several of my interviews and, exceptionally, a few men were old enough to recall the 1912 Minimum Wage dispute and the lock-out of 1921. Interviewed in 1966, John Steer (b.1890) even remembered the Denaby Main evictions of 1902/03. Many of the men interviewed did not find it easy to get a job during the inter-war years, a period that John Steer aptly called the 'Wicked Thirties'. More recent and very clear memories of the 1984–85 miners' strike have also been included. One of my most moving interviews was with Cortonwood's Mick Carter (b.1943), who was ever-willing to talk frankly about the origin and course of the longest major industrial dispute of modern times and, despite his terminal illness, provided information of more than local interest.

My interest in oral history began in earnest in the early 1980s when I started researching my family history. Coming from a mining family stretching back over four generations, it was a natural process for me to record several relatives from mining backgrounds but I wished I had done more. The following project started three years ago when I began to carry out recordings to supplement material gleaned from documentary and printed sources. This commission from Wharncliffe Books of Barnsley then gave me an opportunity to proceed in a more systematic and more extensive manner. Most of the recordings were made from 2003 to the early part of 2005. Sadly, ten of the men interviewed have passed away before publication was possible, perhaps underlining the importance of their testimonies.

In order to assist the reader a **glossary** of mining terms, relevant to all the transcripts, is avaiable at the end of the book. For some terms I am grateful to my mining friends for their interpretation but any errors remain mine.

Most of the recordings took place in the homes of the former miners where I could not have been made more welcome. It has been a great privilege to meet all of them. Tommy Henwood was interviewed in Bentley Miners' Welfare and I am very grateful to the club and his friends for their help and encouragement. Four interviews took place in the Dearne Valley Venture premises at Bolton-up-Dearne when I was tutoring a local history class there. I am grateful to the staff and class members for their support during this period. The previously unpublished interview with John Steer was carried out by his son-in-law, Jack Wrigley. I am grateful to Jack and his wife, Betty, for giving me permission to use relevant extracts. Arthur Nixon, who lives in Norfolk, did a 'self-recording' for me, speaking into a cassette recorder. I very much appreciate his co-operation. Barrie Dalby was kind enough to refer me to Ted Lunness and Eric Crabtree. I am grateful for his interest and assistance.

In most cases transcripts of the recordings were provided for the interviewees and their families and relevant changes, usually minor, were made. Initial interviews varied from about 40–80 minutes and most were recorded using digital equipment. The transcripts reproduced here are edited versions. However, I hope to be able to deposit my original recordings and papers in the National Mining Museum for England, at Caphouse Colliery, near Wakefield.

A series of audio cds under the theme of PIT VOICES, has been published containing short extracts from several of my original recordings.

I am grateful to Steve Kemp, National Secretary of the National Union of Mineworkers, for writing the Foreword and also to his colleague, Ken Capstick, for his help and encouragement. Thanks are also due to Professor David Hey, Dr Margaret Faul and Ian Winstanley for their positive comments about the project. I would also like to express my appreciation to Michelle Winslow from the Oral History Society for technical and general advice. In the latter stages of the project Barnsley area Councillor Len Picken, himself the subject of an interview, has been very supportive, as has Jim Gladman and his colleagues at Raleys (solicitors) of Barnsley. Former Barnburgh miner Bill Bennett kindly allowed the use of his excellent artwork to illustrate the title pages of the four main sections of the book. Copies of these limited edition prints (and several others) can be had by contacting Bill on 01709 896200.

Special thanks also to Matt Blurton at Mac Style Ltd, Chris Sharp of Old Barnsley, Norman Ellis, Alice Rodgers and to all at Wharncliffe Books.

Notes
1. *Useful Toil*, Allen Lane/Penguin Books, 1974
2. Opening and closing ventilation doors
3. A sub-contractor, master miner: also see **Glossary**

Len Picken *and the North Gawber banner, Barnsley Town Hall.*

I
Born Before 1910

'ALMOST TIME'

(1) John ('Jack') William Steer

Born: 19 November 1890
Place: Clifton Street, Carbrook, Sheffield
Pits: Waverley & Tinsley Park collieries, Sheffield
Mining experience: c.1906–1958 (c.52 years)
Age at interview: 76

What follows is based on an interview with Jack Steer carried out and recorded by his son-in-law, Jack Wrigley, in 1966. It provides us with a fascinating insight into working practices and working conditions in the privately-owned era of coal-mining, set principally in Tinsley Park, one of the less well-known of Yorkshire's collieries, before the Great War. Jack also recalled the hardships associated with the national strikes of 1912 and 1921 and, as a boy, he could even remember the ruthless evictions of miners and their families at Denaby Main in 1903. By the time of the 1926 strike he was an official, responsible for safety at Tinsley during the entire dispute but we have a vivid account of what he referred to as the 'Wicked Thirties' when most miners were on short-time and living in extreme poverty.

Studio photograph of Jack and Ada Steer, on their honeymoon, Blackpool, December 1916.
J R & B Wrigley

   Jack's first job – when he was still not quite fourteen – was at Jessop's, feeding small bars through the rolling mill, an early stage of pen-nib manufacture. Some of his pals were earning better money working in the mining industry, though, as we shall see, it was by no means easy to get a job in 1906 without some relevant work experience.

   Jack Steer died in 1969 but part of his marvellous testimony, recorded almost forty years ago, is published here for the first time.

"When nationalisation came in 1947 it released the mining industry from slavery."

"When I was sixteen I went for a job at the Waverley Colliery, the other side of Tinsley Park wood. The first thing that the under-manager said to me was 'Have you worked at a pit before?' I said 'Yes, Tinsley Park pit.' I told a lie, otherwise he would not have set me on. I worked there for three months and then heard a rumour that the pit wasn't paying [making a profit] so I asked another pal of mine if he could get me a job at Tinsley Park pit. I got set on there. I was employed by a contractor who was in charge of the haulage system. He paid me from a kitchen window in Ranskill Road. When I first started you had to go filling first [before becoming a collier]. The collier paid you as you worked for him. You got six shillings a day for filling and he would keep what was left over. If we earned £1 I would have six shillings and he would have fourteen shillings. It was his stall. That's how it worked. If your working place was not available or if there was a filler short somewhere the deputy would send you elsewhere. Once I had to stand the market and worked on five different stalls so had to go to five different pubs to get

Tinsley Park Colliery, Sheffield, from a company advertising/correspondence postcard. This pit functioned c.1852–1943. Norman Ellis Collection

my wages. The men made a fuss about this [in about 1914] and there was a meeting and from then on the market men and others were paid in the pit yard.

I went to work one morning and my lamp was 'stopped' [taken away] so I had to see the under-manager. I thought I had done something wrong but he told me that he wanted me to take charge of the pit bottom [as a traffic manager] and that I would be better-off financially, paid a half-shift extra a week and a shilling for every thousand tons got out in the morning and for every 950 tons in the afternoon. It was a responsible job as all the pit depended on it.

I was two years as a collier and paid my fillers six shillings but I also paid their stoppages, usually a shilling or eighteen [old] pence, so as to encourage them. It was hard work. I wore a pair of pit pants, nothing else apart from shoes as it was so warm, especially when you were working. The sweat ran down my chest. I've seen colliers take their pants off [also see pp 37–9] and wring them out. There was no shot-firing, it was all pick and shovel work.

Before the 1912 Minimum Wage Act, the miners applied for eight shillings a day for eight hours' work. The owners turned it down. Before the Act if I was a collier and had a filler working for me and we were working in a bad place we might fill just seven tubs in a day. I would have to give the filler six shillings but would only have one shilling left for me. I've seen men come home after a week's work with only fifteen shillings. The filler had security but the

Hand-holing, under-cutting the coal with a pick and using sprags for temporary support. Rev. Francis Cobb

collier had not. The lowest seam was the *Silkstone*, about 4' 6", the *Haigh Moor*, *Barnsley* and *Wath Wood* were, on average, about five foot, except of course for the *Thin Coal* but this was not started until after the Minimum Wage Act.

Every collier had his own way of getting the coal. It wasn't just strength as you used your brains. An experienced collier would cut out one side, cut underneath and over the top but a strong man might just use brute force but would achieve less. You would work on your stomach, spragging the coal to hold it up and then knock the sprags out and the coal would fall. When cutting you had to lay on your side under with room to swing your pick. You kept putting sprags under, until about five foot, then knocked them out and it was then easy coal to chuck on. This was the old method of 'holing' as they called it. Siskol machines were eventually introduced, about 1924. Shot-firers would fire in the roof – not in the coal – in the main roads as the roofs had to be ripped down and and built up on each side. This happened at night. With mechanisation the coal was undercut for 200 yards but there needed to be two loose sides so you could fire it. Boring holes in solid coal would result in little coal coming down unless there were two loose ends, for the coal to give.

The pit ponies worked sixteen hours a day.They used to go out at six in the morning for the day shift and stay on at the end until the next shift until ten at night and then had eight hours rest. Sometimes the ponies could not eat their food properly because of blackclocks.The horses put their noses in their food and blew through their nostrils, to blow them away.They tried using gypsum, lime and water [to get rid of them] but it made no difference.Someone had a brainwave. Six holes were bored and filled with powder one weekend.The blast and the reek afterwards killed all the insects.

I was in the 1912 strike which was about the minimum wage.They did not get the eight shillings that they wanted but six shillings and nine pence. We were on strike for six weeks. There was strike pay for the first week and then married men fetched loaves for their children. They had to owe rents. At Denaby, in 1903, the owners evicted the miners from their houses [the Bag Muck Strike] and they had to live in a communal tent, with their wives and children. The coal owners even paid someone to cut the ties of the tent.

The next big strike was 1921 when the coal owners shut all the pits down and the miners had to go in on their [the owners'] own terms. Their terms were reduced wages. No negotiations. So we were out for twenty-one weeks. I was married and had a bit of money put away. I did a bit of outcropping in the latter months. Earl Fitzwilliam put a stop to it in Tinsley Park wood because it was on his land. Everybody was clamouring for coal – householders and industrial concerns – so horses and carts were going into the wood and taking the coal out. It was well organised. The little carting contractors paid the outcroppers.

In the 1926 strike a similar thing happened in some places but I was an official by then so was not on strike. The miners were bitter with the other unions – the transport workers and the railway workers. After ten days the railwaymen went in and the miners were left on their own. It was a losing battle. It was silent revolution due to reduced wages. There had been upheavals in every industry since the war. The workers did not forget and were not as dumb as some think. 'When nationalisation came in in 1947 it released the mining industry from slavery', was a comment said to me by an old miner in Endcliffe Park. He was right. It was the best thing that happened to us. During the war the coal owners could not do what they liked, so the end [of privatisation] had really come in 1939.

The year 1932 was a bad time for the mining industry. A filler got eight shillings a day, so he had only gone up two shillings since 1914. The pit was on a four-day week which meant a

32 shillings wage but you could get 32 shillings from the Labour Exchange. It was wrong. Miners were on the poverty line and unemployment was widespread. The Tories had brought in a means test so that if a man was out of work … and he went for national assistance they came to his home and he would have to sell his goods … before he got any benefit. People were on the the poverty line in the Wicked Thirties, until about 1936/37. It was very bad in Sheffield, especially for families with children."

(2) John 'Jack' Bailey

Born: 24 December 1900
Place: John Street, Wombwell
Pits: Houghton Main; Mitchell Main
Mining experience: c.1915–c.1924 (c.10 years)
Age at interview: 102

I met John Bailey in his Wombwell home when he was 102 years old. John had a variety of 'spare time' jobs even before leaving school, from washing an old man's feet for a penny to helping deliver groceries from a horse and cart and working in the small family shop. His first official job was washing bottles at Wombwell glassworks but he soon left as his mates were earning a couple of shillings a week more at the pit. His father, Paul Bailey, had, like many others, migrated to Wombwell from Staffordshire, attracted by the prospect of work at local collieries. Paul was not afraid to speak up to the bosses but suffered accordingly, sacked as 'unsuitable' because of his opinions, a reputation that did not help young John getting a pit job. In this extract John describes the Bailey family's terrace house, recalls the miners' strike of 1912 and

working at Houghton Main and Mitchell Main, bravely coming out of the pit to work in the blacksmith's shop. He left mining for a job selling insurance, when in his early twenties, after marrying Elsie Thorpe. John's subsequent employment in the Housing Department of Wombwell Urban District Council was interrupted, at the age of forty-three, by armed service. During the Second World War he was deployed in Publicity and Psychological Warfare, meeting Field Marshall Montgomery on several occasions. A remarkable survivor, John is now in his 105th year.

"… we walked miles in old workings and districts long abandoned."

Centenarian Mr John Bailey enjoys a joke and certainly does not look his age (102) in 2003.
The author

"There was a kitchen where we lived [22 Marsh Street] and there was the house [living room], and there was a big area at the back. There were two bedrooms. Four lasses were in one bedroom and five lads in the other. Bathtime was every Friday and we all got in the same bath water. Mother kept heating it up with kettles on the fire. We had our ears 'syringed' by mother every Friday, whether we needed it or not! [laughs]. We left to live at 14 Station Road, opposite the Working Men's Club door and had a shop there. Mother used to make ice-cream and I used to stand from ten in the morning until eleven at night, apart from meals, selling ice cream. I had to go down to the railway station and fetch a block of ice that came from Grimsby every Saturday morning, and pulled it up the hill to the shop.

I remember the national miners' strike of 1912 and all the misery. I would go to Lundhill pit tip picking coal for home use and for my grandparents. We were like a lot of moles scratching for bits of coal. If you were lucky you would find some big pieces but sometimes some big boys would take over and steal your coal. One day my pram load of coal was knocked over and the coal taken by bigger lads.

When I was fourteen [c.1914] I went for a job at Houghton Main. Goodness, I was 'in the money'. I had never seen a pound note before. When I went for the job a chap called Bradbury was the overman and he said 'What do they call thi father?' I told him and he then said 'I can't find thee a job!' I had to bear my father's mistakes.

 I was a pony driver and worked at a place called Number Sevens, about three miles from the pit shaft and one day the roof fell in on the main road that brings the empties and takes the full tubs. We got to know that we could not get out of the pit because of the roof fall. This lad, Conway, and his dad, worked in the same district as me so the deputy got us all together and he wanted the oldest man which was Mr Conway and the youngest boy which was me. There was a stream of them all following us, some with no lights and we walked miles in old workings and districts long abandoned. I wondered if we would ever get out. I was crying and frightened. We would sit down and have a rest. At the front I noticed something in the distance. It was some help, rescue men came and found us. We could see their lamps a long long way away. We flashed them and they came to us and gave each of us a blanket and got us out of the pit and I walked home from Houghton Main to Station Road.

After finishing at Houghton Main, father took me to Mitchell Main. I was about fourteen and a half and we saw the under-manager, Mr Thompson. I was scared stiff of him. He had a loud, bossy voice. I finished up working down Mitchell's pit, my father pleading for me to get set on as he had six kids to look after. It was terrible work. One day I came out of the pit and told my father that I was not going down again. I saw Mr Britain in the pit yard and asked him if he could find me a job on the pit-top. When I told him it was me who brought groceries from my grandmother Dook's shop he told me I could start in the morning. That influenced his decision!

I had a lousy job on the pit-top. I was motty-hanging. Each miner had motties which were for the tubs that were weighed on the pit hill, checked by one working for the miners union and one for the bosses. There was a pile of motties on a heap. It took me all day to see to them. I also worked on the screens. It was a rotten job. A chap from Darfield was the 'bummer'. He went to chapel but he was a lousy boss. We could never do anything right for him. He shouted at us but did not swear, forcing us to do things, for instance, if some of the belts halted he would find something for us to do while it was being repaired. There was no rest. Eventually, I got promoted and got in the blacksmiths' shop and became a blacksmith's striker. I got proficient at shoeing horses. When a horse at lost its shoes underground and my mate wasn't there the foreman said to me, very politely, 'Can tha do it?' I said 'Yes' and I shod two ponies down the pit by myself and from then on I started making shoes."

(3) Arthur Clayton

Born: 27 June 1901
Place: Hoyland Common, Barnsley
Pits: Hoyland Silkstone; Rockingham
Working experience: c.1914–1966 (52 years)
Age at interview: 99

I was introduced to Arthur Clayton for the first time by David [later Professor] Hey, one of my lecturers at Matlock College in the late 1960s. Arthur's knowledge of the mining industry and the local history of Hoyland and the surrounding area was extraordinary. Recently retired from Rockingham Colliery, he was tutoring local history classes at Kirk Balk School and continued to do so for almost seventeen years. Our meeting was the start of a long friendship which lasted until Arthur's death, at the age of 101, in 2002. Arthur came from a mining family, his brothers Wilfred, Friend and Fred working at local pits as did his father who was a deputy and member of a mines rescue team. Arthur had an excellent memory and his

Arthur K. Clayton, BEM. The author

responses to my questions were punctuated with typical anecdotes and stories, interspersed with a good deal of humour. In the following extracts we hear of Arthur's boyhood memories of the eventful two years before the outbreak of the Great War. He proceeded to describe some of his early working experiences at his village pits, Hoyland Silkstone and Rockingham, where he worked for a total of fifty-two years. The transcript concludes with Arthur's memories of the 1926 strike and his impressions of several legendary miners' leaders. Arthur Clayton was honoured with a British Empire Medal in 1988 'for services to English Heritage'.

"We were like young ponies, let out into the grass ..."

"I was at school during the 1912 miners' strike but I am not sure if my father was on strike as he may have become a deputy by then. The children who had not had a breakfast had to come to the front of the class and they were taken to the Salvation Army and they would get a breakfast. I remember the royal visit to Elsecar in 1912 [George V & Queen Mary]. We got a school holiday for it but we went bathing at Elsecar reservoir instead, then went to the pit a bit later. I can remember being in a field by the reservoir and a charabanc went by and someone said that's the rescue party going to Cadeby as there had been a big explosion that day [9 July, 2 explosions, 88 fatalities]. Herbert Cusworth, an under-manager who lived near me, was killed.

I knew several of the men who were killed in the Wharncliffe Silkstone disaster [30 May 1914] – our local pig killer, Jack Fisher, was one of them. He was a well-known village

Hoyland Silkstone Colliery in the early 1900s. Sinking began here in 1874, the Silkstone seam *reached in January 1876. New owners, the Newton Chambers Company, closed Hoyland Silkstone in 1928, its status reduced to a service pit for nearby Rockingham.* Norman Ellis Collection

character. He sang comic songs. There was a boy called Bob Siddall; and some Brays from Hoyland.

I was thirteen when I started work at Hoyland Silkstone in 1914. I went to call on a Catholic lad called Joe Brennan. I lived next to the bottom house in Kay Street. He was a few months older than me. We walked to the pit for the afternoon shift and he left me. He went up a ladder and disappeared in a cloud of steam … We did not report to anyone but we had signed on. I got into this place [the screens] and it wanted John Milton to describe it because it was Miltonic! It was dim and dusty and noisy and there was a little man in charge of us. He had been a teacher but lost his job, through drinking. There was a big belt, really iron plates, which went round an hexagonal thing [and] at the end that fitted the iron plates … … there were some big mechanical riddles … bump bump bump … you could not see for dust. As it came on the belt, a boy stood at the bottom of the big riddle. He had a long rake and would spread it along the belt and there were boys on either side, picking dirt out and throwing it over their shoulders to a place at the back which had a trap door leading to the wagons … A little Irishman was in charge. When you were day dreaming and not picking dirt out he would shout 'I will cut your liver out and put it back and swear I never touched yer'. Later, we used to laugh about it, when some of us had retired, I bet he was more frightened than we were.

With my father being a deputy I then got a job in the check office, handing checks out to the men and weighing carts (horse & carts, there were no lorries) that came for coal, for the colliers. Chalked or painted on the side would be the tare and when it went over the weigh you subtracted that. If he had too much on you had to throw … [with] a big collier's shovel – at that time was a hundredweight – a rough measure, so so many shovel fulls were thrown off or on if he was short. At 4 o'clock, one of the few people that bought coal arrived. It was twenty-five shillings a ton, best coal, Silkstone Coal, Hards as they called them. I used to have take this book, and a tin box with a few pounds in up to the cashier's office.

I was fourteen years and eight months when I went underground for the first time [at Rockingham]. I think I was too young to feel frightened … I was curious to know what it was like. We had a steam winder which was not quite the same as an electric one. After so many [winds], on full steam he shuts the steam off or it regulates, only full steam for part of the stroke. You could feel it pulsating and all the boys said that when you got half-way down you felt as though you were coming back up.

My first job was lamp-carrying, getting four safety lamps from the lamp room on the surface and taking them down the pit, walking a long way, from Rockingham towards Skiers Spring, with a lot of other boys and men. During the shift, if some colliers 'lost' their lamp – there were no electric lamps, apart from the manager's and under-managers' – I had to swop them. They frequently went out. Just a jerk would do it. The pony driver would bring it out and when I got two, what we call 'dark' lamps, I had to swop them for two 'light' lamps and then I had to walk back to the pit-bottom. You could not open your safety lamp without it going out. Sometimes you fell down and they all went out and sometimes big lads would clout you and take the book off you and write all sorts in it. I did this for a few weeks and then went pony driving.

It was a bit strange working with ponies to begin with. All the new lads had Dan because he ruled himself. He was a small pony and would do anything. There were some bad ones but I never got the worst ones. One was called Snap. It used to stand and kick, breaking all his gears. There was a shaft that fitted round the pony, the chain on it and this thing that fitted on to the truck and you dropped this long pin through it and that coupled it to the truck but on rare occasions two or three boys were killed when it jerked out and they fell and the trucks ran over them. You used to sit behind the pony, like a drayman. We sat behind the pony with his legs between the dray and himself on these limmer shafts, keeping your head down on haulage up to the colliers, three empties at a time and bringing three full trucks back. Accident to ponies? Well, the head stableman for the whole pit used to come and kill them with a 'peggy'. I never saw it done. While it was on the floor, they would hold two or three safety lamps before its eyes … and they would suddenly remove them and let bang. I often saw them come past me on a long tram.

I was in the *Parkgate seam* … in the King Coal but after perhaps eighteen months I was put on the haulage, endless rope haulage, not far from the pit-bottom and worked there for a number of years, where there were two roads where we got a lot of coal off. The coal came here and down a drift to the pit-bottom and I worked at the top of that. There was three trucks on this endless road haulage, every ten or fifteen yards you hooked three full trucks on and at the bottom they were doing the same. The full trucks pulled the empty trucks up. A chap called a tomier or a corporal [was in charge]. If you weren't used to it you finished up running for an ambulance man, fingers trapped.

After the [First World] War there were several strikes, lasting a few days or a week or so and there was a national strike in 1921. I remember walking by Bullhouse Hall and the colliery was working. It was a little drift mine. I said I bet they did not know that there was a strike on. There were places for children to get food. I spent a long time walking and bathing in Elsecar reservoir in 1921 and 1926: there used to be hundreds there. Men learnt to swim during

An underground photograph of Arthur Clayton working the tandem bunker, Rockingham Colliery, c.1964.
Author's collection

strikes. I remember going down to Elsecar in the 1926 strike and there was a little man called Chad Walker who was a lot older than the others. They were laughing as they were walking down, it was a sunny day and they were saying, 'We're going to duck old Chad when we get down' and he had a bathing costume which would have fitted Fatty Arbuckle. They would all rush down together into the water. Old Chad went under and he was twenty yards from them – he could swim like a fish! I can't remember any picketing but we went coal picking on the huge muckstack near the station, off Sheffield Road. It was from a pit, according to several generations of local people, that produced the best house coal in Yorkshire. We were like young ponies let out into the grass, we did not have feelings about the owners [laughs]. I should not be living now were it not for those two strikes. It lengthened men's lives. There were no holidays with pay. We even walked to Bamford and Hathersage [Derbyshire], coming back on the train. We had nothing else to do. We had no bathing costumes but if we came to some water we would still bathe. The bellman would come round and would announce that the union had been given some money and there would be a voucher for five shillings for us to use at the Miners' Institute.

I can remember Herbert Smith coming to Hoyland Common [Working Men's] Club and telling them that he had been to a meeting and that he was kept waiting in a room and

Several of Arthur Clayton's friends and neighbours toast his 100th birthday, Kay Street, Hoyland Common, 27 June 2001.

someone said, 'Mr Baldwin's come' and Herbert replied, 'I know, I can smell him.' It is no good being a union man unless you are not frightened of anybody. I don't mean physically frightened. He was known as 'Herbert Smith' and not 'Our 'Erb' as is generally thought. This was a journalist's phrase. He wasn't as clever a man as Joseph Jones who was a great speaker. He would have his handkerchief in his coat tail and it was worth £100 to see him put his hand round his back for his handkerchief [laughs]. I heard A J Cook speak twice. Once at Tankersley [Miners'] Welfare Hall, from the balcony, and once at Thorpe [Hesley]. There were crowds at Thorpe, in an old army hut. We had walked there [from Hoyland Common], having no money. We were one of the first to arrive and three or four men were around a big iron stove inside and a man called Tom Higgs who was a lot older than me, commented, 'Look out chaps, there's mutton warming itsen.' You see they called Thorpe 'Mutton Town'. The story was that someone stole a sheep there and when the constable went searching it was put in a cradle and wrapped it up but just when he was leaving it went Baa and it was found. Yet there is a not about that time in the Wentworth estate records offering a reward for information concerning a stolen sheep at Thorpe. Cook was late arriving so someone asked Joe Randell 'to do a turn', He was a little chap and a Communist who had been to America and was well read and could speak but when he got up you could not get him down! We then heard some clogs rattling outside, men coming from the pit, still working! Someone shouted, 'Look through the window Cookie!' "

(4) John Willie Clamp

Born: 28 September 1901
Place: Sherwood Crescent, Rotherham
Pit: Manvers Main
Mining experience: c.1915–39 (c.24 years)
Age at interview: 103

I interviewed John Willie Clamp at West Melton Lodge Nursing Home, shortly after his 103rd birthday. Their most senior resident, he was able to recall some aspects of his childhood and early pit work during the Great War. His first job was as a 'deputy-lad' at Manvers, when aged thirteen or fourteen, progressing to pony driving and haulage work. John Willie's mining career came to an abrupt end about the start of the Second World War when the *Barnsley seam* in which he was working had become exhausted. Later, he found employment at Parkgate Forge, Wath Brewery and, ultimately, for the Council's water board, retiring at the age of seventy.

John Willie Clamp, who had recently celebrated his 103rd birthday, West Melton Lodge Nursing Home, 12 October 2004. The author

"... he sat me down and left me in the dark!"

"I was born at Sherwood Crescent in Rotherham but I came to live in Wath when I was five years old. My father, John William Clamp, was a pit deputy at Manvers. I was named after my Uncle Hugh who went to America as a gentleman's valet. I had two brothers, Joe and Isiah, and two sisters, Lily and Agnes. My grandmother came to stay with us before she died. She was born in Scotland and her father looked after the royal estate at Balmoral. Granny used to see the Queen [Victoria] riding around on a pony.

I attended Victoria School until I was fourteen. I was a champion runner, a 100 and 220 yard sprinter, and won lots of competitions. One of my first prizes bought me an overcoat.

My first job was at Manvers, working in the *Barnsley seam*. I had had a medical examination for the army but they would not pass me as I was having treatment on my face. As soon as the pit manager knew my name I was given a job. I wore shorts and had clogs on my feet. I was on nights on my first day, working as 'deputy boy' and had to walk round with him but he sat me down and left me in the dark! I went to sleep until he came back.

I started driving ponies and then became an haulage hand. It was hard work. I had to pull this rope off the engine. It was an old fashioned engine, pulling the tubs halfway to the pit-bottom. I had to knock the tail rope off and hang it on to full 'uns to go half-way home. I started to drive the engine myself when one of the blokes left.

I remember some wage disputes. Once, coming out for more money, we all sat outside the lamp room, waiting for the verdict before agreeing to go down afterwards."

23

(5) Tommy [Thomas Patrick] Hart

Born: 29 January 1905
Place: Burtonwood, Lancashire
Pits: Grange (Droppingwell); Warren House;
Kilnhurst; Aldwarke Main;
Roughwood; Barley Hall
Mining experience: c.1918–1970 (c.52 years)
Age at interview: 98 & 100

I first interviewed Tommy Hart in November 2003 when he was ninety-eight-years-old. He made me really welcome at his Herringthorpe home, showed me an air-raid shelter that he had built in his garden during the Second World War and, apart from responding really well to my mining questions, also talked to me about his long association with gardening, his interest in sport and great passion for coarse fishing. My second visit took place two months after he had celebrated his one-hundreth birthday. Tom continued to be in fine form, recalling, in a clear and distinctive voice, many aspects of his exceptionally long life. The following edited extracts are based on both interviews.

One-hundred-year-old Tommy Hart proudly displays his birthday card from the Queen and his photograph on the front page of the Angling Star, *celebrating the catching of a large carp, 8 April 2005.* The author

"... in those days you could leave school at thirteen."

"My hundredth birthday fell on a Saturday. I had 128 birthday cards and it was beautiful to receive a card from the Queen. The Mayor and Mayoress came to see me. A hundred people, family, relations and friends attended a special celebration for me on the Sunday and everyone had a great time which I appreciated. My son-in-law gave a speech and I responded – and it was brilliant. The Mayor and Mayoress came to visit me on the Saturday and on the following Thursday I was taken to Clifton Park Museum which had just been renovated and I was the guest of honour, at the opening the new healthy eating restaurant.

My father came from an Irish farm in Galway. He worked at Bickershaw Colliery, a damp Lancashire pit and, when I was three years old, died from pneumonia through working in water. When I was thirteen and half, in 1918, I became an orphan as my Mother had also died in the influenza epidemic, so I went to live with my sister-in-law at Kimberworth. I was taken to Droppingwell pit. If you had enough attendances in those days you could leave school at thirteen. The only place to earn a living was at the pit. I walked there from Kimberworth – there were no buses, and got signed on to work on the pit-top, loading props into the tubs. I looked forward to going underground and, with me being in board and lodgings, I needed the money. I was filling wooden props into tubs. I got £1.5s pay and I had to take my check to the window and I would be given the money in a numbered tin.

In 1921 when I was sixteen I went to Warren House pit [after the miners' strike] and stayed there until 1935 when it closed. My first job was unlinking tubs. There would be eight or ten tubs, linked together and pulled by the haulage rope. I was in the pit-bottom area. There was a steam boiler where you could put your bottle of tea and keep it warm. I took bread and lard or dripping for my snap. I was told not to take meat as it would give you indigestion – but this was a bit of a joke really, as nobody had got any! There wasn't much choice. My snap was wrapped in paper and you hung it up until it was snap time. I had two big pockets in my waistcoat. In one pocket was my bottle and my snap was in the other, perhaps with a couple of apples.

I did a lot of pony driving at Warren House pit [Wentworth Road, Upper Haugh]. They called it John Brown's Number 2. There were about thirty-six ponies there. Some were named after First World War battles such as Verdun. All the coal went underground and came out at Aldwarke Main as that was where the railway was. Ponies were well looked after. They would walk [on their own] into the stables and go into their own stalls. It was unbelievable, you did not have to guide them. Sometimes they could be awkward but I never got kicked. I remember that we rode them. I got on top of the pony and laid down so my head was below the pony's head but we did not do it a lot. The stablemen, though, were very strict and would inspect every horse and pony and you got a clip around the ear if there was something wrong. You called them 'Mr', not by their first names.

When I was nineteen I knew that if I got a tramming job it would increase my wages and help me towards the time I would get married [Tom married Rebecca, they were both twenty-one]. One day the under-manager, Mr Dalton and Mr Hotchkiss, the manager, were passing and I spoke to the undermanger and asked him if he could find me a tramming job and he replied, 'Eh lad, I couldn't find thee a tramming job even if tha gave me a gold sovereign.' Mr Hotchkiss, asked me how old I was and I told him. He said that there would be tramming job for me on the Monday. I was sent tramming with one of the union men. There were three men working on the coalface, two colliers and the trammer who was the man who filled coal into the tub … the colliers were the two men who got the coal with hammers, chisels and picks..the trammer filled it and brought it out from the coalface, shoving the tub along little rails for the pony driver to take it away. You put your oil lamp on your neck (but you also wore a scarf as the lamp would burn you). The pony driver took it away, one tub at a time depending on the incline. If you were a good trammer and there was a collier short you might get his job and get better pay. But there was a gang of spare men and if any place needed a spare man they would take their place. There was about six inch of solid slurry under the seam of coal and I had to dig it out with a pick, throw it away. At first I made a lot of grunting noises just like a modern tennis player but he [the collier] told me stop making the noise, and to just keep chopping at it and it would still break up. Some men might work in several different teams so he had to go to several paying outs to get his week's wages. There may be six men, working in different areas, and all the money went on one card. The money was divided in a pub, after one of the men had collected the money. It was put on the table and shared out. A trammer got paid five to four. The trammer was the apprentice, he was learning the work, so if the collier got fifteen shillings the trammer got twelve.

I then went to Kilnhurst Colliery but there were buses running then and I had a bike then. War started when I was there but I decided to move to Aldwarke Main as I thought conditions would be better there. Mr Hart lived in Clay Pit Lane and his son was called Tom, a contractor to pits at different places. He had a contract for Kilnhurst pit and a deputy called Ernest

The Second World War air-raid shelter that Tommy Hart built in the garden of his Herringthorpe home was still in good condition when I visited him in November 2003. The author

Cotterill told me he could get me a job at Kilnhurst. So I went and got signed up to Tom Hart and his son, Tom Hart, so there were three Tom Harts and an Ernest Hart in a team! We were in the stone. It was a drift. When they were short of a collier they used to fetch one of us but I became more and more in demand, so I became a regular face-worker. Two Bevin Boys worked with us, two lovely lads from Bristol. One of their fathers had a big yacht. They said that when the went back to Bristol they would describe how hard the work was down the pit, earning every penny you get.

I left Kilnhurst for Aldwarke which was a good pit. You went down the shaft and then down a drift to get to the coal … down the Dalton drift … you could even hear Silverwood workers and their machines.

I left Aldwarke for Roughwood in 1949, in the Kimberworth Park area, a drift mine, known as the 'Happy Pit' as everyone was comfortable there, there were no disputes. I was there until it closed.

In 1926 when we were on strike it was one of the hottest summers, it was beautiful. We had bread and lard and no money. A lot of spare time but no money and not much food. They were bad old days not good old days. Herbert Smith, who always wore a cap, was a good miners' leader but I think that Arthur Scargill was the best because he won a lot of compensation cases for Yorkshire miners, cases that otherwise might not have been brought to justice.

I was off work twenty-nine weeks after breaking my femur. I finished up working on the pit-top at Barley Hall where they were very good to me, allowing me to do a variety of jobs."

26

(6) Gerald Booth

Born: 21 October 1909
Place: Barugh Green, Darton, Barnsley
Pits: Dodworth & Redbrook
Mining experience: c.1923–74 (c.51 years)
Age at interview: 95

Gerald Booth holds the framed certificate marking his '60 years faithful service as a local preacher and lifetime service to Barugh Green Methodist Church,' 5 May 2005. The author

Gerald Booth is a senior member of the Barugh Township Local History Group where I met him on several occasions. He is a respected and well-known Methodist, with preaching experience going back to the 1930s. Gerald's entire working life was spent on pit-top tasks, starting on the screens at Dodworth and finishing in the relative comfort of Redbrook colliery baths. Surface mine workers often had hard and dirty jobs with less pay than their underground counterparts but their labour and skills were essential for the running of any successful colliery complex. In this extract Gerald describes some of his work experiences and also talks about his lifelong interest in his local chapel which, of course, included Bible study and plenty of singing. It was marvellous to hear Gerald's rendition of one of his own compositions as well as a superb interpretation of a favourite hymn. Gerald became an accredited preacher in March 1934, serving for sixty-four years, when he was ninety.

"You had to pull them [tubs], shove them, sort them ..."

"My father was called Titus and mother was Jane Harriet Anne Senior. I had a brother and four sisters. Father was a collier, working at several local pits and at Dodworth, retiring at the age of seventy-two but died within a week. He had to fill a stint of 12–13 yards a shift. He drove headings at Dodworth. Latterly his job was cleaning up by the side of the belts, when coal would spin off. I attended Barugh Green School and then Higham School until I was fourteen. I was told not to go to the pit, to get an office or shop job but there were no shop jobs apart from the Co-op and then no vacancies. I went to Dodworth pit with my cousin, Alan Booth, after the Christmas holidays. They only had two days off in those days. The pit-top engineer told us to go into the office and we signed on.

I wore short trousers but soon needed some long ones, and had clogs on my feet – they stood some hammer and the irons on the wooden soles could be replaced. I picked the shale out and threw the muck between the spaces [on the screens]. I worked with Ben Lockwood, who had a wooden leg, but travelled to work from Hoyland Swaine on a bike. He would show me what to pick. Conditions were terrible with all the dust and it was cold. One lad who had

Full wagons at Dodworth Colliery in the early 1900s. Chris Sharp/Old Barnsley

ginger hair wanted to fight and one day jumped on the belt, really they were metal sheets, and kept saying 'Stick 'em up'. I got fed up of him so I grabbed him and knocked him off. Ben didn't half laugh. It was a day-wage, 13s. 7d. a week at fourteen and a shilling rise each birthday. Saturday was pay-day. We went to the pay-office and received our money in little tins after handing in a pay check.

After about a year I went on the pit-hill where the tipplers were. They were like big bobbins. You put the tubs in and pulled a lever and the coal dropped out and went on the shakers where there were riddles and the biggest coal went forward and there were more riddles for the rest. When you got to sixteen, notices were usually sent out saying that if you did not go underground you would be finished. Most lads went down. Mother and my sisters did not want me to go down the pit as there was enough with my father and my brother, Henry. I continued working on the creepers, the bottleneck of the pit. From three shafts the coal came up from the *Flockton*, *Wharncliffe* and *Parkgate* seams. There were two weighs and the coal went up the creepers, to the top, the highest point, where there was a square landing and inside were big motors for driving them. There were 6,000 tubs coming up per shift. You had to pull them, shove them, sort them – it was very heavy work. Sometimes they would get fast in the rails and everything would stop. It was a nightmare at times. One winter I came home with a long cut on my hand but sewed it up with needle and cotton. I did the job for twenty-three years.

There was an aerial flight at Dodworth and the stone that came out of the pit, from areas which were made by the rippers, was carried away and emptied into a big pile, a muckstack. The pit-hill foreman told me that I could not have a job there so I went to Woolley Colliery and handed in my notice. I had a family of six to keep. The manager at Dodworth asked to see me.

He told me that I could start on the muckstack tomorrow, though it would not be a job that would last but said that he would find me something once the job ended, so I accepted and stayed there. On the muckstack I took a snap tin which wasn't really big enough as I took ten slices of bread and jam, what I called 'fruit sandwiches'.

My next job was at Redbrook, when a borehole was sunk, about twenty-one inch in diameter, and shale and muck was sent down. There was a big belt for the muck which was blasted by compressed air into the gobs. I worked there about eight years. The engineer then came to see me one day and asked me if I was interested in a job in the Redbrook baths. I told him that I did not work on Sundays [because of chapel attendance] but he said that he could get round that. My brother, Henry, worked in the baths as he had had a serious injury in the pit. The job included scrubbing the floors and tiles after the men had showered; also sweeping up and swilling away all the muck. The baths were heated by a big boiler which had to be kept fired up. It made steam which went all around the baths. It was the best job I ever had, away from the bad weather. When I had some spare time I was able to read my Bible and prepare for preaching. Someone might see me and say 'What's tha reading?' I told them that they could not find a better book. I also did some singing. Fred Rideough also had a good voice. He worked in the medical centre. We sang a lot of hymns. I wrote some hymns and we would try them out. A tune would come to me and I would put words to it.

I started going to the chapel when I was three years old. My Mother was a very keen Methodist. I would attend Sunday school and two or three services on the same day. We also sang hymns around a piano that Mother had bought. I became interested in preaching. I met a famous Methodist preacher called William Challenger who was an inspiring character. He would preach in the open air. I heard him several times. People rallied round him as there was no chapel then at Kexborough so they met in the barn of the White Bear. Challenger converted a lot of people.

Gerald and twin sister Geraldine, a studio photograph dated 18 August 1932. Gerald Booth

The chapel anniversaries were always popular. We had to have extra seating for the Sunday school children. There was a big harmonium. Whitsun was also a special time. We went around singing in the village and later on walked around Higham and Barugh and Dodworth. Sometimes I got the Salvation Army band from Cudworth to lead the way. After we had walked we would sing hymns and had a tea and there were games. It was a grand time.

I have written several hymns and they have been sung in the chapel, some as solos, some for together. Here is part of one that I composed in the style of *The Happy Wanderer* tune:

> *I love to go to Sunday School and lift my voice in praise.*
> *And hear the Bible read out and to learn about God's ways.*
> *Praise the Lord!*
> *Bless His name,*
> *Shout for joy!*
> *Let us lift our heads and voices in God's praises*
> *Praise the Lord!*
> *He is worthy of our praise!*

One of my favourite hymns is *When I Survey the Wondrous Cross* [sings several verses, to the tune of *Monte Christie* in a fine and clear voice]."

A happy group of people in Barugh Green Methodist Church. Gerald Booth

II
Born 1911–1920

127
500

'ALL CLEAR'

(7) Tom Emms

Born: 24 November 1911
Place: Callow, Chesterfield
Pit: Yorkshire Main (Edlington)
Mining experience: c.1925–1974 (49 years)
Age at interview: 92

When farming was on the decline in Norfolk William Frederick Emms (Tom's father) found work at a colliery near Chesterfield, owned by the Staveley Iron & Coal Company. The Emms family moved to Princess Crescent, Edlington in 1912 where over a two-year period (1909–11) Staveley had sunk Yorkshire Main. After leaving school at the age of fourteen Tom found employment at his father's pit. He also had three brothers who worked there, so there were five miners in the family. In this extract Tom describes how he got 'set on' at the pit and his first jobs. We also hear how he progressed to become a deputy, a role that he kept for thirty-five years at one of Yorkshire's biggest and most productive collieries.

Tom Emms in his bungalow at Warmsworth, 21 May 2004. The author

"I wore trousers buckled at the knee ... it was cold in the pit bottom!"

"I had no idea what I was to do but the pit was the only job to go to. There were no other jobs. I was fourteen on the Thursday and on the Saturday morning my father took me down to the colliery to see the clerks and the under-manager and I signed on. On the following Monday I was at the pit at 5.30 in the morning. Father had bought me a pair of pit boots, I wore trousers, buckled at the knee [bannickers], long stockings, a vest, shirt, coat and a cap – it was cold in the pit-bottom!

Mother put corned beef or jam sandwiches in my snap tin for my lunch. Jam was appetising in the pit, it was refreshing. I attached the tin to my belt and away I went. There were no pit baths in those days. When I signed on they gave me a check, so that was fastened to my belt as well. When I handed it in I was given a lamp. Alfred, my brother, took me to the pit-top, then on to the cage and down the pit. As it set off down when I got half way it felt as though I was going back up again. It was a double-deck cage, twenty-five to thirty on each deck. They looked after me. When I got to the bottom my brother told me to sit there for a while while he reported to the deputy who took me to the corporal, the man that dished the jobs out, and he set me on clip-carrying. These clips were put on the ropes and pulled the tubs to the districts, and back again. I was dragging clips and chains from one end of the shaft to the other. As they were bringing the coal in I sent the clips out to send the empties back in, to bring the full uns to the pit-bottom again.

I did the clip job for about four weeks and then I was sent coupling the tubs together. As they came off the cage I had to couple them up, the empties. I was still at the pit-bottom and did that for a month. At the pit-bottom, by No.1 shaft, it was very cold but in No.2 shaft, because the air went round the pit, down one [shaft] and up the other [shaft], it was nice and warm, warm air coming from the districts. They set me on, learning with these clips that I had been carrying, learning to put them on the ropes and on to the tubs. I took them off the empty tubs and sent them out full but the clips were heavy to handle and carry. I learnt the job in three or four days and did it regular.

After I had been working about six months the strike started, on May 1st 1926. I was fourteen and a half and went coal picking on the tip and brought sacks home to keep the fires going. I did this until November when the strike was over. My father had a pony and cart and did various jobs to survive. There were soup kitchens at the school, for pupils with no food; also money came from Russia and every miner got half a crown. I also sold coal for pocket money. It was a relief to get back to work.

I then went on to rope running, taking empties to the coalface and bringing full ones back, with a long rope worked by an engine at the top of the gate. It was a matter of seeing that the clips had been put on properly and if there had been a smash you had to sort things out. I did this for three or four years until I was eighteen. I was then made a corporal, like my brother.

By the age of twenty I had already got a lot of mining experience but I was kept on the haulage until I was about twenty-two and then one of the managers came round and told me that he was looking for young officials. I was asked if I would consider becoming a deputy. I had not done very well at school but I was told that I would be taught how to go on. I was asked to go to Edlington night school and Doncaster Tech for the examination which I passed. I was twenty-seven or twenty-eight.

This postcard of Yorkshire Main was used on 26 September 1923, not long before Tom Emms started work there as a pit-bottom lad. Norman Ellis Collection

First of all I was a 'pit bobby', going round the face and checking for any 'hidden' props which were valuable items. I had to find them and tell the men to dig them out. I carried a 'bulls eye lamp', with a bright light that shone a long way. You could spot a prop in the waste where a man had laid it down. I did this for six months and then was trained on the face and became a deputy. I started on the Mid-West in the *Barnsley seam* which was five foot six to eight inches. It was hand-got to begin with. It was a beautiful seam, you could shovel the coal straight into the tubs. I used a pick and had a go at filling.

I had a lot of respect when I was a deputy. I always asked the men questions and they would give me questions and that's the way I got on – learning their way and they learning my way. I had forty-five men to look after on a shift. I set the men off, with my book, six front rippers, six tailgate rippers, fourteen to sixteen putting packs in, men boring holes, cutter men and so on.

Yorkshire Main was a very good pit, with a big workforce and we produced a million tons three or four times during my time."

(8) John [William] Williamson

Born: 15 June 1912
Place: Great Houghton
Pits: Houghton Main
Other NCB employment: instructor at Askern Training Centre/Wharncliffe Silkstone No 5 Area & Barnsley Main; Divisional Consultation Officer; Director, Divisional School for Minerworkers (Doncaster); Recruitment Officer (North of England & Scotland); Assistant Manpower Office (No 5 Area), Grimethorpe
Mining experience: c.1926–1960 (44 years)
Age at interview: 91

John William Williamson outside his bunglalow at Darfield, 22 February 2004. The author

John Williamson has had a great deal of experience in the mining industry, both below and above ground, starting as a fourteen-year-old 'nipper' at Houghton Main. As a child he had suffered a physical disability, a tubercular left leg, but he was able to tackle a wide variety of underground jobs. John told me that he was determined 'to better himself', so went on to attended evening classes and qualified as a deputy. Interested in work with young people, he left the industry for a short period and qualified in youth leadership, working in Marlow, Buckinghamshire. When John returned to mining he worked as an instructor, at the National Training Centre, at Askern Colliery. After the Centre closed John was transferred to a small training unit in the Wharncliffe Silkstone (No 5) Area, working with trainees from all over

Britain and from overseas. When Whancliffe closed John was moved to the Barnsley Main Training Centre where hymns were sung before going underground. Further NCB appointments followed, servicing committees and, when Yorkshire pits were needing more manpower, John had the responsibility of recruited men from northern England and Scotland. In his final post, as Assistant Area Manpower Officer, John was based at Grimethorpe. The following extracts, relating to his early mining life, are based on a recorded interview and John's autobiographical writings.

"... I walked about a quarter of a mile with the older chaps, tripping over everything I came across."

"As soon as I was fourteen I was told, 'You had better get down to the pit lad, they are setting men on.' I went there on my own and knocked on the manager's or foreman's door. I was asked my particulars and who my father was. As soon as I told them that my father and grandfather were miners I was accepted and I was signed on as a 'nipper'. I had to change from short trousers to long ones and could walk fairly well by then. I went to the pit for five in the morning. The first time I knocked on the lamp room door and the man said, 'What does tha want?' so I said, 'I've come to work here,' and he said 'Who are tha?', so I said 'Johnny Williamson' and he said, 'Oh aye, that'll be thi number... and here's thi check. Tha teks this wi thi wherever tha goes and when tha comes out tha gis it me everyday, then I know thi's out.' From then on I was a miner! I was given a CEAG electric hand lamp which had recently been developed, but it weighed 7 lbs. I was only 4'6" so the lamp dangled from my leather belt, knocking my knees. I soon got used to it. I wore clogs on my feet. When we went to work they would say 'Clogs are going!' I wore a cloth cap on my head.

Going down the shaft was a bit strange at first. I was told to stand in the middle, there were fourteen of us on one level of a three-decker cage. We used to go down in forty-five seconds, slowly to start with, then there was a 'whoosh' and we were down. From the pit-bottom I walked about a quarter of a mile with the older chaps, tripping over everything I came across. The seam was on a gradient, so the level roadway was cut through the seam. I had to walk up this rise or go down a dip to the workings. I was given a piece of steel with a hook on the end and was told to hook the rope and then walk up the side and and pull it down so the tubs could get up and down. A man showed me for the first five yards and then left me on my own, to keep walking. When I got to the top another young man showed ne how to pull the blocks across the road so the tubs could be lowered on.

A tub was like a box on 4 wheels and carried 8 cwt of coal. They would go up empty and come down full. It was in the *Parkgate seam* which was hot, dry and dirty. During my first week two men were killed. One of them lived at Wombwell and Herbert, who was working near, was called to take a blanket and lay it over the dead man – a terrible thing for a lad of fourteen to experience.

Next, I was given the job of a water carrier and I had to travel from the pit-bottom to the coalface [where it was very hot], right to the far end, twice a day, with a tank of water on four wheels. I would fill it with water at the pit-bottom and take it to the men at the coalface. They [the fillers] would fill their bottles and dudley's, seven pint dudley's which they carried on their backs. As a nipper I carried a two pint water bottle for my own use, and hung it with my clothes. I was told that oatmeal water was best so used that for quite a while.

I got promoted when I was seventeen-years-old and became a haulage driver. A rope from it would pass around a pulley and down along the roadway and down the dip. They would couple this on to twelve tubs and would signal me to pull them out. Sometimes the tubs could not be pulled, the roads were always dirty and and the roof was always falling down. On one occasion I could not get the clutch over to the other drum so the tubs came straight across, through the engine house, knocked out the front supports and all the roof came down. I was stuck for fifteen minutes while the men outside shouted, 'Are you all right, Johnny?' and at the same time cleared away the debris so we could continue with the work. The engine was so powerful that I could only hear the bell ringing by feeling the vibrations, resting my head on the bell. I did this job for a few months and then the *Parkgate seam* was closed down.

I moved to the *Meltonfield seam* [aged sixteen or seventeen] and became a pony driver. It was low and wet. They gave me the best pony of the lot, called Potch. I was told 'Tha mun fetch Potch out, he's in't second stall.' I walked down to the stable and wondered what on earth I was meant to do to gear him up, but old Potch had been there so long that he knew the job better than anyone. He eased towards the side so that I could put gears on him and he even put his head through the collar. I have never seen anything so daft in all my life. From time to time I

A young pony driver collects his horse from the stables. Notice the animal's protective leather hat.

got an awkward pony. In the 4′6″ seam the weight would come on it and the roof would sag a bit so the tubs were just scraping through and ponies of normal size could not travel, so they had two ponies which were small, like big dogs. One, called Tiny, was built like a racehorse but so small that a tall man could stand with his legs astride him; and the other pony, Tunny, was as stout as an elephant. If he did not want to move then that was it! You could be dismissed if you abused a pony but, sorry to say, some were knocked about a bit. Most men were kind to them, bringing treats and bits of snap. At some pits in the [holiday] seasons some ponies would be brought out and there would be pony races.

I then became an haulage hand, lashing tubs on to a moving rope in the *Meltonfield seam* but at the bottom of a 1 in 3 drift, almost straight up! If tubs went up then they certainly came back fast and I was at the bottom! I had a little recess to escape into if there was a runaway.

When I was nineteen I moved to the coalface. It was the start of the machine-age, with electric undercutting machines in use. I was a filler but started as an 'apprentice' or what was known as a 'trammer', working alongside an experienced man. My job was to go there after the machines had done their work and the coal had been blasted, kneeling with a shovel, loading the coal on to a conveyor and using my pick to get the coal that had not come out after firing. I worked a seven and a half hour shift with a twenty minute snap time. My snap was bread and dripping or jam and a bottle of water. Gran would wake me up with a shout, usually several shouts, each getting louder, at 4 am. My snap would be waiting for me, wrapped in the *Daily Herald* which was a working man's paper. I would meet my mates at the end of the street and we would walk a mile and a half to the pit."

(9) Tommy Henwood

Born: 30 October 1911
Place: High Row, Loftus, Cleveland
Pit: Bentley Colliery
Mining experience: c.1925–1975 (c.50 years)
Age at interview: 91

It was on 20 November 2003, when I attended the Bentley Colliery Commemoration Service [for those who lost their lives in the 1931 explosion and 1978 paddy train accident] at Arksey Cemetery that I first met Tommy. He was a very deserving and regular guest of honour at the service, laying a wreath at the very moving ceremony. Later, I was able to interview him in Bentley Colliery Working Men's Club, and met him there, along with his friends, on a number of subsequent

Tommy Henwood was in a sprightly mood when I first met him at the Bentley Memorial Service, Arksey cemetery, 23 November 2003. The author

occasions;and also at his home, and, sadly, in hospital, just before he passed away, in November 2004.Tom was proud of his Cornish roots, his paternal grandfather and father being tin miners. The Henwoods moved to Bentley via Cleveland. In the following extracts Tommy recalls his early days working at Bentley Colliery, often near or alongside his father, including one occasion when he continued working naked, despite a VIP visit of the Lady Mayor.Tommy also spoke, with considerable emotion, about the Bentley disaster of 20 November 1931 when, in the immediate aftermath, he worked as a volunteer pony driver, providing us with, probably, the last eye-witness account of the dreadful occasion when forty-five men lost their lives. Tommy was one of a group of Bentley pitmen who were recruited during the Second World War. He saw distinguished service in Italy and fought at the Anzio bridgehead where he was wounded and later hospitalised.

'I was working naked and my father told me that the Mayor[ess] *of Doncaster was coming down the pit ...'*

"I started on the screens when I was thirteen. My first [underground] job was feeding tubs into the cage in the pit-bottom ... lockering up, running three tubs of coal into the cage. I then went catch knocking, pulling coal in and running empties [tubs] round and then I helped with rope splicing. I also went pony driving. The deputy said 'There's your pony.' I asked him what

Tommy Henwood was a regular guest of honour at the Bentley Memorial Service, paying tribute to his former workmates. The author

they called him and he said 'Bob'. He said that I was going round the pit-bottom with the pony to get used to him. I only did that for a day or two and then I was told to take my pony and go to the New North East where my father worked in the stalls. I did not have any problems with my pony but I had some problems with the others. I used to ride them [but] the deputy used to stand with his lamp out with a whitewash brush and splash us.

I went from the pit-bottom into the districts … I got a shilling a day … My dad was the chargeman, paying us in the pit yard. I worked on the 'buddy' system until I was twenty-one.

I am the only miner at Bentley pit who had the Mayoress of Doncaster wringing out my pants! I was working naked and my father told me that the Mayor and some women were coming down the pit, so put my pants on. But I refused. He told me he would belt me when I got home but I still refused. So the Mayoress came down. I thought that she needed to see what the miners had got to put up with. I said that if she wants to turn her head away, she can go back up the pit. The manager asked me to put my pants on when they arrived. I said I would not. The Mayoress said, 'That man is naked!' Dad told her that my pants were hanging up to dry. She went up to them, took her gloves off, and she wrung 'em out! They were soaking with sweat.

I worked in the New North East face, a *Barnsley seam* which was 5'6". You had to fill a stint of coal off. I used a pick and shovel, hammer and wedge and a ringer [long bar]. At the bottom, by the floor, we put wooden blocks under and took the coal … and knocked them out and put wooden props up so we could get cover and then knock the props out and the face would come down. If the props didn't hold then you got out of the way. I have been buried up to my neck

Tommy Henwood, pictured with some of his Bentley Miners' Welfare friends at the commemorative pulley wheel in Bentley park. They are, left to right: Melvyn Tomlinson, Allan Armstrong, Tommy Henwood, Harry McMahon, Peter Falconer and Wilf Gibson, May 2004. The author

but when mechanisation came, steel props came in. We preferred timber as they would split and crack and warn us.

I took Cornish pasties for my snap, made by my grandmother, two pasties in a snap tin, cut in half. It was a joke for the men. They swopped me with their sandwiches. I had a four-pint dudley of water.

I [remember] the Bentley disaster.... I was with my father ... and I had just finished work when the explosion happened. It was a Friday evening. I was on days. They said that there had been an explosion at the pit and they were asking for volunteers to go down. My father went down. They asked for pony drivers so I went down and got my pony. I was told to take sand bags, not very far from the pit-bottom. We got to the district where the explosion was. The air was turned round with the blast, reversed. I was told to go towards it as in a couple of seconds it would go back to normal. We had a right [bad] time of it. My pony would not go but I never hit him. I told him to go in his own time and all at once he set off and pulled the tubs with the sandbags, taking them to where they were needed and I unloaded. I then loaded them up ... I never touched the bodies but saw them. My father told me to take them to the pit-bottom, and to hurry up back with more sandbags. He was doing some running about. I told him that I was also running about and he was working me to death. He told me that I would pull through. From the pit-bottom the bodies were taken up to the ambulance room and then into the church. I came out of the pit and went to have a look around and I thought that there were one or two blokes that had been missed ... there was one bloke still in the pit, one of my relatives, [Henry] Womack. And that is why this club has given me the honour of laying the wreath for the Bentley miners in front of the Mayor. I knew Tommy Hopkinson, the ambulance man. He was a good man but lost his life. It was crowded at the pit-top. I attended the funerals at Arksey Cemetery. I had to come out of the church the first time, it was just too much for me."

Tommy enjoys a drink and a joke with his friends in Bentley Miners' Welfare, May 2004. The author

(10) Harry Taylor

Born: 17 May 1913
Place: Shepherd's Rest, Barnsley
Pits: Rob Royd Colliery; Church Lane [Dodworth Colliery]; Monk Bretton Colliery
Mining experience: c.1927–1966 (40 years)
Age at interview: 90

Harry Taylor spent his early life at Kingstone, near Barnsley, within walking distance of Dodworth collieries. The oldest of seven brothers, pit work was expected of Harry, his wages essential to the family income at a time when his father was abroad, a professional soldier. In this extract he describes his early days in mining at Rob Royd, working as a pony driver and on the haulage. We also hear about Harry's move to Dodworth's Church Lane site where he worked as a trammer. Later, Harry found work at Monk Bretton Colliery, but his mining career was interrupted during the Second World War when, off work sick, he

Harry Taylor outside his bungalow at Kendray, Barnsley, 1 March 2004. The author

was 'dragged into the navy'. Not to be deterred, Harry's abilities were such that he achieved Petty Officer rank, serving on HMS *Ark Royal*. Like most miners, Harry had a number of outdoor leisure interests, which he talked about during the interview with great enthusiasm.

"The pony knew better where to go than I did."

"I left school at the age of fourteen in 1927. I left school on the Friday and went to work at Rob Royd Colliery on the Monday, straight underground, and my first week's wage was 17s 3d. I got the job there because all my uncles and relations worked there. I only had to tell them that I was able to start on the Monday. I looked forward to it. I knew everyone that worked there. Going down the pit did not worry me as pit life was common chatter. I always walked to the pit from Kingstone.

On my first day I waited at the box hole in the pit-bottom and someone said, 'What are you waiting for?' and I said, 'I've started today.' A man said 'Come on with me, I'll show you where to go', and he took me down to

Harry Taylor made the most of his unexpected call-up to the Navy, serving on HMS Ark Royal. Taylor family

the stables where a young fellow was getting a pony ready. I was told to go with this lad today, stay with him, and come back with him as that would be my training. Tomorrow my job would be to take the pony out myself. That was the procedure. You put his headgear on and there was a strap on its back with a tail chain to couple up to the tubs to pull. The pony knew where to go better than I did. You walked behind it. There could be three or four ponies going. When you came back the same thing happened again. You had to undress the pony. It only pulled one tub at a time but it was a steep incline. Each set of men that were filling tubs used to take the tub into their working place themselves and when you fetched it out you took the pony into the maingate, coupled it up and brought it out. When there were so many tubs of coal a line was used to an endless rope, there was a signal and it was pulled to the pit-bottom. Some ponies were better than others. One pony would not stop with anyone else. We always gave them treats, filling our pockets with grass from the fields. There were pit pony races held at the Queen's Grounds and the ponies had a couple of weeks off for respite, during [Barnsley] Feast Week.

Rob Royd was a small pit but a good pit. After pony-driving for about twelve months I went 'jinnying'. One set of full 'uns would would be coupled up together at the top of the jinny [hill], up to twenty of them. At the other end, at the pit-bottom, were the empties. Rope went round a pulley wheel at the top. When you knocked the block out in front the full 'uns used to pull the empties back up. I once caused a runaway. I thought everything was coupled but … half the load went down the jinny on its own. They tried to fine me 7s 6d but my Dad went to the pit to protest as I only got fifteen bob a week.

Next, I went to Church Lane [Dodworth], to get a copper or two more pay, working as a trammer. I worked there when we used to share a note. I worked with a collier. If we got fifty bob a week we did well. Everything was hand-got. You went into the pass-by and got empties and shoved them to where you filled them. There would be a collier and a second man who filled the tub … that was your job all day: taking empties out and bringing full ones back. For tramming you got paid a bit more than the normal rate, as the second filler paid you. There were three of us and the usual procedure was to have five or six bob a day.

Eventually, I went to Monk Bretton pit. I shared on a note there, as a trammer, to start with. I then filled coal on to a conveyor belt on a face. I had a stint of coal to fill, all shovelling. The majority of the coal was fired and cut but there were some difficulties. I started in the *Beamshaw*. There was also the *Kent seam*. Some of the coal was thin … just a couple of foot. We laid on our sides or we were kneeling. You had so many yards to fill.

While I was at Monk Bretton filling coal someone suggested that me and my mate should go somewhere to pass an exam to be a deputy. I passed first time. I took my certificate to management and asked if I could get promoted. Within a week I was a deputy. My weekly wage was then £7. It was a terrible responsibility, with twelve to fourteen men under me. I got on well with them though there were occasional differences and plenty of humour such as 'Look out, the deputy is coming'. I started at five-thirty [am] so had to be up at four.

I saw a bloke killed one day at Monk Bretton pit. I was in the maingate showing someone how to do something when a man was working at the head of the face. A machine cutting the coal killed him. I was called immediately to the scene. For leisure I had a lot of interests. I

Left: An early photograph, c.1900, showing the sturdy timber headstocks and brick steam-winding engine house at Rob Royd Colliery. Michael Hinchliffe

Harry Taylor, like many miners, had a variety of sporting interests, including the game of bowls. Taylor family

used to fly pigeons. I have flown miler birds at Kingstone and Measbrough Dyke. I have had some good miler birds. They flew straight and low and very fast. There was a lot of betting. It was five bob a bird to enter and there was a different place each week. From Kingstone we used to fly from Dodworth, from the cemetery and from Worsbrough Common. The venue was drawn each week. I also kept greyhounds and raced them at Dillington Stadium, Worsbrough Common. I had one, called Trinity, that beat them all. It was good money. I also played nipsy and knur and spell and I have had a passion for playing bowls."

(11) George Ronald Rawson

Born: 7 July 1913
Place: Church Street, Royston, Barnsley
Pits: Wharncliffe Woodmoor 4&5 (Carlton Main); New Monckton; North Gawber; Monk Bretton; Dodworth (Redbrook)
Mining experience: 1927–1975 (48 years)
Age at interview: 91

George Rawson can often be seen in Barnsley's Central Library, meeting and chatting to friends in the coffee bar. His autobiographical writing, lodged in Local Studies and Archives, under the title of *My Boyhood Days*, includes splendid anecdotes about growing up in the mining communities of Royston and Carlton. George has great affection for the long period that he spent at Redbrook section of Dodworth colliery where he became a popular deputy and overman. Late in his employment, following a knee injury in a shearer accident, he was placed in charge of the pit-top Delay Control Room, a job which

George Rawson and his deputy's lamp, Barnsley, 9 December 2004. The author

he admits was 'boring' compared to his underground duties. He retired, aged sixty-two, after almost half a century in the mining industry. A committed Christian for as long as he can remember, George has now been a preacher, particularly at Measbrough Dike Evangical Church (where his son, Philip, is Pastor), for almost seventy years, an astonishing record.

"If we rode ponies we got into trouble."

"I can remember the 1921 pit strike. The Superintendent in the Salvation Army was George Griffiths, who became Royston's MP as part of the Hemsworth division. He was a Welshman and was a great supporter of the miners. He taught us a little ditty which we sang:

> *Nothing to Pay*
> *No, Nothing to Pay*
> *Straight is the Gateway,*
> *Narrow the Way*
> *Free Breakfasts in Royston*
> *And Nothing to Pay*

I can also remember the great pit strike of 1926. I went to the soup kitchen in Carlton Methodist Church. To raise funds people organised events such as garden parties and concerts; and comic bands paraded through the village with begging tins.

Working on the pit-top screens was a typical first job given to many young miners. Author's collection

I started work at Carlton Long Row pit [Wharncliffe Woodmoor 4 & 5/ Carlton Main] on 12 August 1927. My job was to pick dirt out of the coal on the screens. I wore shorts and old clothes. The screens were large iron conveyors on which coal came out of the pit. It was tipped down chutes by tipplers. As the coal passed us boys, we had to pick the dirt or muck out onto this big conveyor belt. At that time of the day the cleaner the coal was then the more money the owners could get. There was a big lad from Monk Bretton who used to stand at that side of the conveyor and every now and then he would pick up a piece of coal and break it in two, and he said that is what I am going to do with you. I thought he might be making me a chicken so one day I said to him that we had better have it out, after the shift. We struck a blow but someone came along and sent us home. I'm glad they did because I would have lost! Next morning we got to the pit as usual but when we got to the pit gate Mr Bray, the pit-top boss, was there. He called to us and we had to take our caps off in respect in those days and call him 'Mr'. 'You were fighting in the pit yard, weren't you yesterday?' 'Yes Sir' we replied. He told us to go home and tell our mothers that he had sent us home for fighting at the pit. As we left the big lad said he would not tell his mother but I said that I would tell mine.

Father came home from the pit one day and told me that he had got me a job working with him, at Monckton, as a pony driver. I was fourteen years and three months. I had to report to the box hole in the pit-bottom and the deputy would tell me where to go that day. I walked out to the stables where Mr Silcock was in charge. He was very keen and really did look after the horses. When you got back at the end of the shift he would examine them to make sure that there were no cuts, bumps or bruises. We put their collar on and the harness or gears which were hung up in the pass-by. The chain, which was about five or six foot long, was hooked onto the tubs. The miners would fill the tubs by hand and take them to the pass-by. My pony was called Midget, it was the smallest in the pit but I was only small too (5ft 2 inches). It was well-behaved and intelligent but it would not stand still while I put its gears on at the start of the shift. Sometimes the ponies would catch their backs on the roof so the deputy would send repair men to dint the floor and therefore lower the roadway. Later, I had a pony called George, the same name as me! That's when I went to work with Uncle Harry and Jim. If we rode ponies we got into trouble. Every so far down the main roadways there were manholes, where you could go for safety. The stableman might hide in there, with a brush and a bucket of whitewash, so that when the pony drivers rode past they were splashed, so there was no excuse when they got to the pit-bottom. They then got a telling off from Mr Buckle, but if you did it too often you got something stopped off your wage – and that meant more trouble at home!

When I was eighteen I became a haulage engine driver. The tubs went on to the pass-by via the main and tail ropes, driven by compressed air. I suffered an accident. At the end of the shift I had to turn a big valve off which supplied the engine with air but it hit me in the face. I was carried out of the pit and was in Beckett Hospital for three days. I still have problems with my jaw.

At this time a lot of the coal at Monckton was 'hand-got'. Four men worked a pillar of coal or stall, two on day shifts and two on afternoon shifts. They had to hew under the coal with picks. There was no shot firing. After holing under the coal, by lying on your side, iron wedges were driven into the top of the pillar of coal to make it leave the roof, then the coal was broken up with a sledge hammer. One of the hammers was bigger than the other and called a 'Monday' as no one liked using it after a weekend off. The coal was then filled into the tubs, a motty was put on the tubs (or a chalked number) and the tubs were taken by the pony driver to the pass-by where they were sent to the pit-bottom by the rope haulage. Hand-filling and hewing was very hard work.

By the time I was twenty or twenty-one [1933] my family moved from Carlton to Smithies. I went to the Mining College and got my papers for shot firing and deputying. Mr Cyril Weaver, who attended my chapel at Smithies, was the manager of North Gawber Colliery. He told me he would set me on with some drift miners for a while and then appoint me as a shot-firer. I was not too thrilled though when I saw what was happening there because I was a sticker to rules, in fact I became known as 'Mr Systematic' and I did not like the way they carried on there, especially with explosives. It's a wonder one man did not blow the pit up! The faces were low and they had just started using machine-cutting. They had a Siskol Tupping Machine which cut into solid stone. It looked like a big machine gun, mounted on a tripod, and driven by compressed air. I worked worked with some men cutting a drift into the *Haigh Moor seam*. The tubs were lowered down the drift by a self-acting rope haulage or 'Jinny' as the men called it.

There were pit baths at North Gawber but they were really just showers. There was a big room with pulleys and ropes with several hooks and you got undressed, hung your clothes on the hooks and pulled them up. My first pit-head baths were at Monckton where there was a clean end and a mucky end. We came home in our muck when I worked on the screens. You did not bath at home daily, miners would not wash their backs daily as they thought it weakened their backs. Mother would have a big piece of hessian, like sacking, which was rubbed on his back. They bathed once a week, in a zinc bath which was hung on a hook outside the back door. No one pinched them! Another superstition was that if a man was going to work and he met a woman he turned back as it was bad luck, someone might be killed that day. There was only woman who was allowed to pass miners in the village, called Mrs Greenwood, who was the midwife. That was OK.

I can remember the 1936 disaster at Carlton [Wharncliffe Woodmoor 1,2&3 colliery] on 6 August. I preached my first sermon the same year, in Smithies chapel. My old Superintendent at Sunday School, Herbert Hall, was one of the victims. I knew a lot of the men who were killed. I went to the memorial service held outside the front of Barnsley Town Hall but the streets were so packed I could only get as far as Regent Street. Reverend Luke Wiseman conducted the service. It was very upsetting.

After North Gawber I had a short spell at Monk Bretton Colliery but only for a few days. I decided to come out of the pit and work on the pit-top there and was put in charge of the boys on the screens. I had been warned that 'Costa' Skelton, who was the manager, was difficult to work for. On this morning I could see him leaning on the railings, looking down on the screens. In a while he came down and said, 'Tha not driving these lads[enough]'. I told him they were doing all right and they kept the place clean. He said 'Does tha know who tha talking to?' and I told him I did. He said that he could sack me so I asked him to write me a note out and would finish, which I did.

I was on the dole for a couple of weeks but I met Harry Pickering, an overman at Redbrook Colliery. He knew I had my shot-firing papers and he asked me to come and work at Redbrook which was known as The Happy Pit. It was a good place to work. We even had an underground carol service every Christmas [1949 to c.1964]. I would lead the prayers. Harry Pickering, the pit overman, was also involved. Like me, he was also a local preacher. David Balfour, who conducted our singing was the organist at Dodworth Wesleyan Reform Chapel, and Arthur Hoyland was our chairman. We all worked on the nightshift and clubbed up together and the men's wives would make cakes, mince pies and so on. The man who led the singing was Mr Cooke, the violin player (who was a shot-firer and the sole instrumentalist). We had mince pies afterwards. We always enjoyed the carol services which had the blessing of our manager, Mr Norman Schofield."

(12) Bernard Goddard
Chartered Engineer, Fellow of the Institute of Mining

Born: 6 January 1917
Place: Brook Hill, Thorpe Hesley, Rotherham
Pits & Responsibilities: Grange Colliery: screen lad to under-manager (1931–47); HMI of Mines & Quarries for Northumberland, Durham & Cumberland (1947–52); Manager: Rockingham Colliery (1952–55); Group manager: Area 5, Group D (Barley Hall [formerly Thorncliffe]), Grange & Smithywood (1955–62); Production Manager, Area 5 Yorks Division (1962–67); Chief Mining Engineer, Barnsley Area (1967–69); Head of Production, Doncaster office (1970–1975); Director of Mining Environment, NCB Doncaster & London (1975–80); Mining Consultant, MSA & NCB (1980–90)
Mining experience: 1931–90 (59 years)
Age at interview: 87

Bernard Goddard had a highly successful and extraordinarily long career in the coalmining industry. When meeting Bernard it was fascinating to see examples of so many mining mementoes, and awards that he has received from all over the world.

One of six sons of a Thorpe Hesley miner, Bernard started work on the screens at Grange Colliery at the age of fourteen, but was soon tackling a variety of underground jobs. Through ability and a great deal of application, he moved through the ranks to obtain under-manager and manager's certificates when still in his twenties. Crucial to this progress was his attendance at evening and day classes under the guidance of Rotherham college principal, Geoffrey Dix and colliery manager, John E Longden. In 1947, still only thirty-one, Bernard was appointed as an HMI for the Northumberland, Durham and Cumberland areas, the youngest mines inspector in Great Britain. Over a five-year period his duties included attendance at many inquests, several major explosions (Weetslade, Choppington A, Easington and Eppleton) and incidents; and he was the chief prosecution witness in the first case brought against the NCB. Moving back into production was an unusual step, but Bernard was never one to dodge hard work and face new challenges. His experience and abilities as a manager

Bernard Goddard photographed in his Thorpe Hesley home with his manager's lamp and a specially carved stick presented to him by the NCB's Chairman, Mr Derek Ezra, April 2004. The author

and senior manager were certainly recognised by the National Coal Board. He became a chief spokesperson when the Director of Mining Environment, visited many European countries, North and South America and the USSR. A period of consultancy work followed retirement from the NCB. The following extracts are based on my conversations with Bernard Goddard, his own writings and records.

"... I would be the youngest [Mines] *Inspector in Great Britain."*

"My father, Matthew Goddard, was a miner at Barley Hall pit. When I became an under-manager the manager said to me 'If you become as good an official as your father was a workman then you will be at the top of the tree.' The butty system operated then throughout Yorkshire and Nottinghamshire. Butty men were friends and relations of the senior officials and they allocated the work, so if you took a ten-yard stint, they would take a six, because they said they were there to help out in case of difficulty. My Dad would go down on the first draw (there used to fourteen draws a day) and always came up on the last one. He was filling eight to ten tubs of coal more than anyone else but getting the same wage.

I went to Thorpe Hesley Elementary School and left at the age of fourteen. In the village there were three pits, employing most of the local [male] labour force, then there was Newton Chambers and a few farms, so to get decent money it meant a job at the pit. The reason I went

Bernard Goddard, Thorpe Colliery, 1958. Bernard Goddard

to Grange rather than Barley Hall was because Grange was working 'threes' and 'fours' [days] and Barley was only working twos and threes.

I walked to the pit, about one and half miles, and was interviewed by Mr J E Longden, the manager, and was set to work on the screens, peddling there on a second-hand bike which cost £5 at 2s 6d a week. After six months, I requested work underground as it was better pay. Mr Longden said that I would 'rue the day!' I felt frightened going down the shaft the first time. It was a single-deck cage, holding twelve men. I wore clogs, short trousers, an old jacket and a scarf. My first job was opening the ventilation doors to allow the tubs on the main and tail haulage roads to proceed. On my third shift I accidentally knocked out my flame lamp and had to use my spare one but the deputy, Bill Wright, borrowed my spare for a collier to use on the face, leaving me in the dark for several hours, having to listen to the sound of the approaching tubs. When the manager came round everybody stood to attention and I said to myself, rightly or wrongly, that if I was going to stop in mining then I would try for the top job. I said to my Dad that I had seen Mr Longden, the manager, today and that he had said good morning to me. I told my Dad that I would like his job if I stayed in the pit and Dad told me that there was no harm in trying but it is not easy getting to the top, you need someone pushing you – but I was determined to push myself.

I then went tramming which was hard work, pushing full tubs of coal, each one weighing about nine hundredweight. There was a fatal accident when Stanley Ibbotson, aged seventeen, was run over by tubs. I was once fined 7s 6d when Mr Longden and a HMI caught me riding on the tubs but it was repaid later. I also did some pony driving, taking materials on the the gate roadways to the coalface. If you 'crossed' the horsekeeper he gave you a troublesome pony, perhaps one that moved too fast. If the roadway was narrow and you went to the front the pony would attempt to run you down or would refuse to move if you put on an extra tub. I also spent a year as a surveyor's assistant, measuring and dust sampling, before going on to a variety of coalface work at the age of nineteen. Mr Longden said he would not pay me a penny extra for this but it was good work experience. I was involved in all the tasks of mining in seams varying from 2 to 4 feet or so and under varying conditions such as water, faults, rolls and slips and high methane emission in the *Silkstone seam*.

Whilst at Grange, aged twenty, I trained as a rescue worker and captained the team for three years, and also the first aid team, helping to win competitions and prizes.

I had started going to night school at the age of fifteen, to a local school but was soon attending Rotherham Technical College, on a four-year [part-time] course. Some lads laughed at me, thinking I was wasting my time but I had the last laugh. Several people who helped me: one was Geoffrey Dix, the College Principal, who became my guide, mentor and friend; and Mr John Ernest Longden, the Grange pit manager, who was a great character, the best mining engineer that I have ever met. I did not realise that Mr Longden and Mr Dicks were good friends. I got a note to say that Mr Longden wanted to see me. The only time you were sent to see a gaffer as when you were in trouble so I could not work out why he wanted me. When I got there Mr Dix was present too. At that time if you were trying to improve yourself the officials thought that you were after their job and put obstacles in the way to stop you going to school. I was moved from day shift to afternoon shift which meant that I could not attend classes. I was often told to stay over and do 'nothing a yard' jobs. Mr Dix arranged for me to study in his office at the Tech in the morning. He wrote a letter in red ink to the under-manager and I was put back on the day shift. Mr Longden arranged for me to become a 'working student', learning a variety of jobs.This meant up at five, coal filling, on shifts that could range from six to nine hours, for just 7s 6d a shift. No extra pay or overtime.

I started shot-firing, then went deputying, moved on to become an overman at the age of twenty-two. What makes a good deputy? Well, first of all a man who knows his job and who does not have to resort to obscene language to express himself. I never swore. Lead by example, never let a man do a job that you can't do yourself. I was told that I should be called Mr Goddard not Bernard Goddard when I was an official.

Presentation to a sixty-eight-year-old retiring miner at Thorpe Colliery. Bernard Goddard is standing third from the left. Bernard Goddard

I became an under-manager at Grange, the youngest in South Yorkshire, aged only twenty-three [1944]. I obtained this by working hard and continuing to go to school. The manager's ticket consisted of a written and an oral exam. Mr Longden would occasionally phone me and ask me to come to the pit for a chat on the night shift. Sometimes we would talk about anything but mining but on other occasions it would be all mining.

Bernard Goddard, left, with the Bishop of Wakefield, centre, on a visit to Monk Bretton Colliery in June 1963. Note the large 'contraband' notice at the pit-bank. Bernard Goddard

NCB Chairman Lord Robens, second right, on a VIP visit to Dodworth Colliery, 10 September 1970. Bernard Goddard is third from the left of the group. The buffet lunch looks good. Bernard Goddard

I remember Vesting Day very well [1 January 1947]. Harry Kingston was my recommendation to hoist the flag as he was the oldest workman and a good man. But he did not want the job but I persuaded him. The manager said to him, 'Now then Harry, you know what NCB stands for don't you?' He said, 'Aye, nobody cares a bugger!' The flag had a blue background with 'NCB' in white lettering. If you had achieved your target you flew the flag.

I was up for the group manager's job, responsible for Grange, Barley Hall, Thorncliffe, Rockingham and Smithywood, five pits. Mr Longden asked me why I had not applied and I told him that there were many more people who were more senior than me. He told me that that was nothing to do with it, and to get my application in. I had to go to Hobart House, the NCB headquarters, for interview. Mr Longden, or 'J E' as he was known, did not ask me a question, saying that he knew Mr Goddard and his abilities, saying that if he was not capable he would not be there.

I had taken the written and oral exam for the Inspectorate and had not heard anything but was then informed that I was to be offered a post in Northumberland and Durham and that I would be the youngest inspector in Great Britain [1947]. I was thirty-one. I believe, also, that I was the first man to become a Mines Inspector who was born in South Yorkshire. First of all I was based at Whitley Bay and then Newbiggin by Sea. I went round all the pits and the Coalmines Act (1911) was the bylaw. I did reports every day. I got a 'reprimand' once because I was not taking any holidays! It was a great experience. I attended many [fatal] inquests, several major explosions, inrushes of water and small fires;and was at the first prosecution of the NCB by the Ministry. I carried my gear in the back of the car, as I was so keen, like a bloodhound I was off to the pit. I was often the first inspector at the scene.

In 1952 I decided to move out of the Inspectorate. Promotion was very limited as you had to wait until someone died or someone retired. As a general rule it was unusual for someone in the Inspectorate to go back into production. But that did not trouble me, I was not afraid of the hard work, I enjoyed what I was doing. I went to see Mr J Longden and I was appointed as colliery manager at Rockingham [1952] and then Group Manager and Area Production Manager[1956]. My later appointments with the Board included Area Chief Mining Engineer[1968] and Director of Mining Environment [1975]. I had an office in London and Doncaster and became the chief spokesperson for the Board as we had joined the European Iron and Steel Community. I visited sixteen countries, speaking on behalf of the Coal Board, including Russia which had a poor safety record. America had a very good production record but a poor safety record. I worked with the NCB Chairman Derek Ezra who was a real gentleman. He had a special stick made for me when I retired. I had to send him a monthly report and he always read them thoroughly. I went to Luxembourg every three months, for four years. I worked with Joe Gormley and got on well with him too.

Mining has been very hard work but I have enjoyed my life in the industry."

(13) Ernest Kaye

Born: 24 May 1917
Place: Robinson Terrace, Birdwell, Barnsley
Pits: Rockingham; Wharncliffe Silkstone (Pilley); Houghton Main
Mining experience: c.1931–1978 (47 years)
Age at interview: 83

Veteran miner Ernest Kaye and his wife, Mildred, photographed in his Smithies, Barnsley, home in 2001.
The author

Many of the miners who I have interviewed were able to recall with some detail aspects of their childhood and early days at work. Ernest Kaye was exceptionally lucid in remembering the year 1926 when his father, Albert, was on strike. He also provides us with a fascinating account of how young lads were 'recruited' to a pit and his first underground job as a 'door trapper' at Rockingham Colliery. Later, we hear about pony driving, working on the haulage, working with the ropeman, becoming a 'corporal' (in charge of several men) and working with new machinery. We also hear about an accident that kept Ernest off work for almost a year. 'Lighter duties' followed, in the box hole, looking after the time box and, finally, reporting stoppages when monitors were installed in the control room.

"It was a lonely job [door-trapping]*, on my own all the time."*

"The [1926] strike was 'clog and boot time' if you like, not much to wear, no money at all. There was my mother and father, me and my two brothers, one of them dying aged ten. Quite a few people gave food to the community. We went to school as normal, some were worse than me … wearing just one shoe … big holes in jumpers … we used to take our pot to school and go across the road to Birdwell [Working Men's] Club and have our tea there, two jam sandwiches and a cream bun. At the top of our road there were some allotments and one very knowledgeable chap decided to sink a pit. A big hole was dug. All the men, colliers, stood around and they went as far down as to think they would get some coal, twenty or thirty feet. My dad was among them. A big bicycle wheel with a rope on and a bucket was set up and they used to shout, 'Reight, lower it down'. There was one man in the bottom, filling the bucket who would shout and they would pull it up, empty it on the top and lower it back again. You would pay for that … for two buckets of coal, as much as you could get and everybody would volunteer and take their turn … they used candles for light, for three or four hours at a time. That was one way. The rest of the time they might spend gardening and free seeds were obtained from a firm in Barnsley. Another way later on was coal picking, at Pilley pit. I took a big sack, and would go with my father. It was picked by hand from the muckstack, put in the sack and I was told to take it home, empty it in the coal place and then come back and by the time I came back he would have another ready. I had a bag and would shove the bag of coal through the frame and walk from Pilley to Birdwell. Another day we could be boring from Rockley Wood (permission from Tindale, the [estate] forest keeper [woodman] on land owned by Earl Fitzwilliam. We got permission to saw some trees. I was the oldest so was told to take it home and another would be ready when I came back. We took rope from orange boxes to tie the bag, put it through the frame of the bike and walked to Birdwell, about a mile, and empty it. Mother did a lot of baking. We went to the Co-op with a list and they would then deliver. We never went as far as Barnsley as it would have meant getting a bus.

Dad had been in the pit all his life and his close school friend was under-manager at Rockingham. He told my Dad to bring me to see him at his Hoyland Common home, and he would have a look at me and, if I was satisfactory, would be set on. Dad told me to 'get dressed up' and he took me to see him. 'Now then mester,

Ernest Kaye in short trousers when still at school, about the time of the 1926 miners' strike. Ernest Kaye

this is him', and the under-manager said, 'Oh aye, he's all reight this lad ' and I was told to see so and so. Dad took me to the pit on the Monday. It had been my fourteenth birthday the day before – my details were taken and I was told to report to lamp cabin and so and so would take me down the pit. I was absolutely terrified that first morning, going down in the chair. My oil lamp was on my belt and I held on to the bar, got off at the bottom, feeling frightened to death. I was told to stay with this man on an eight-hour day shift, bank to bank. When I got home Mother asked me how I got on and I said 'shocking'. I had been door trapping. There were big wooden doors, two together since when ytrotmou opened one to go through you had shut that one and open the other so the air was not stopped. I was shown what to do, allowing people to pass through, opening and shutting. I had my snap more or less whenever I wanted, bread and jam or dripping put up by Mother, wrapped in paper and a bottle of water. It was a lonely job, on my own all the time. The air pressure meant pulling the doors hard, using the bar on them, and going through with whoever was passing. I sat on a bit of wood or stood, waiting. I got 2s 10d a day (14p) plus a 'percentage' depending on the tonnage that was achieved.

From there I went to be a pony driver, aged about sixteen, taking empty tubs to two miners and returning with full ones. You went with someone for a start, there were stables for the ponies were they had their food and they were all named such as Spider and Tony. We put the harness on, called sling gears, attached from harness to the back of the pony, which we coupled onto the tubs. We brought him back at the end of the shift, fastened him up and he would have his food, ready for the next day. Some drifts meant about a quarter of an hour walking to the face where there were two or three colliers. Two men turned the tubs on one side to bring the full ones past and I would put it with the pony in the pass-by.

After three or four years I got on to the ropes. Ponies were being phased out and ropes connected tubs to the pit-bottom. Tubs were pulled from the pit-bottom by lashing chains, about a yard and a half long, which we hooked on to them by hand. The rope was pulled by an engine of about 200 hp. The tubs were taken off the top of the jinny and run round into the pit-bottom … empties went down and full ones came back up. It was a steep drift so there was a lad at the bottom and at the top and the engine master. I was an assistant. We got while we could put the chains on while the rope was running but if you missed, it went down without the chain and it was a right do, tubs up in the air, but we did not miss.

I then drove the engine for a while and got to be what was called a corporal, in charge of three or four lads, looking after the ropes, pulleys on the floor, and then started to be a roadman, repairing and replacing the rails and putting new sleepers in with a claw hammer. Tub rails were about four yards long. Sometimes sleepers wanted lifting up, sometimes sleepers needed dinting down.

I did this for two to three years and got a bit better off, more 'man-holing' as they said in those days. I started with the ropemen, rope-splicing, learning at weekends. It was an old miner, George Norcliffe, who knew the ropes well. He used to stand just where rope came off the engine to go down the drift, running it through his fingers and any little strands he would notice and the 'bad rope' would be sorted at the weekend. There were four of us plus old George.

I moved to Pilley [Wharncliffe Silkstone] 'for a better job', where my Dad had moved to. The manager, Mr Wroe, was an old school mate of Dad. The rope was a 'self-acter' that went to the top of the incline, ropes were on the floor and we had a clip which we attached from the rope to the tubs. Weight of the full tubs pulled empties but if the balance was not right it used to stop so we had to go up the drift, swing on the ropes to make the the tubs go. I used to drive the engine as well and had developed a lot of knowledge.

I was courting my future wife and aged twenty-five and her dad said he could get me a job at Houghton when I married [1942]. I started on the ropes, became a corporal and – between jobs – was the onsetter – putting men on and off the chair in the pit-bottom, lifting the gate up and counting the men, dropping the gate and off they went. I also did the jobs of men who were off work. Houghton was a big pit, they called it The Grandfather. It was well run, one of the best in the area. I did all sorts of jobs.

On the face they were changing to a new system using a Panza unit, they were being installed as a trial. On this day they were short of men to put side plates onto the chain that went underneath so myself and my road-laying mate were involved at the weekend. My mate was getting the plates from the gate into the face and I helped put them on with a fitter. I was underneath … when a big lump of coal dropped on my back, knocked me to the face, the Panza still running. I shouted 'Hold it!' to stop the machine and it stopped. I was lifted off. Both my legs were paralysed and I was put in a timber truck to the end of the gate where there was a belt to the pit-bottom, and then out of the pit. I had a fractured pelvis. It was wartime, during the black-out. I was sent to Firbeck Hospital [near Rotherham] for convalescence, over a month, but was off work for a year. I got no compensation."

(14) Fred Elliott

Born: 2 September 1917
Place: Hilda Terrace, Carlton, near Barnsley
Pit: Wharncliffe Woodmoor 1,2 & 3 (1931–63)
Related employment: Grimethorpe Power Station (NCB), 1963–78
Mining experience: 1931–63 (32 years)
Age at interview: 87

Former Wharncliffe Woodmoor 1, 2 & 3 colliery fitter Fred Elliott outside what remains of the old pitbaths at Carlton, 30 May 2005. The author

Fred Elliott, my father, was the third of nine children born to Fred and Susannah Elliott nee Firth. Fred senior is believed to have worked at Dodworth Colliery and, certainly, at the Monckton colliery complex at Royston. Mining extended back further, albeit for a brief generation, with Jonas Elliott (my great grandfather), who worked in coal and ganister pits around Deepcar, near Sheffield, dying from respiratory disease, aged forty-seven. My father recalled been sent by his mother to the yard of the Ship Inn, near Monckton pit, to 'intercept' his dad's pay, in the days of the butty system. The men 'stood in groups and one had a little ready reckoner, with each person paid according to their yardage and number of shifts.' Fred, junior, attended Carlton Board School, leaving at the age of fourteen. In this extract, he talks a little about his parents, and aspects of his work, principally as an underground fitter, at Wharncliffe Woodmoor 1,2, & 3 [Old Carlton] Colliery. Fred obtained a job as a fitter at Grimethorpe Power Station, still part of the National Coal Board, three years before Woodmoor 1,2 & 3 finally closed, in 1966.

"On my first day I went straight underground ..."

"My father was a coal filler on the face. He did not talk much about the pit but was very interested in his pigeons. He used to race them and see to them every day. He started at the Ship Hotel where they used to have their meetings and that's where he used to send the birds to different places and where they were registered and ringed. He had some fine ones. They went as far as France and Spain, flying from Nevers, Rennes and San Sebastian. He once sent four pigeons to one race and they came first to fourth but for some reason the first was disqualified. It was Royston Pigeon Club. He won gold medals.

My mother was a very quiet lady, she never bothered us but she had some hard times with my father when I was young. She did loads of baking. I used to fetch flour from the co-operative at Carlton, two stones at a time, which she kneaded in a big bowl [panchion] which was covered and put at the side of the hearth. She made buns as well as bread, flat cakes, scones, anything really. How I got my first job? We'll, there was an old gentleman called McKenny who worked at the colliery and drove the main underground haulage engine. His check was No.1! He told me to go to Wharncliffe Woodmoor, 1,2 & 3 colliery. On my first day I went straight underground and did catch lifting, in the *Kent*['s Thick] *seam*. I wore old trousers, an old shirt and pullover. When I went down for the first time I got so far and I thought that I was coming back up! Catch lifting, well on the chair when they put the tubs in, there was a lever which you pulled and it released the tubs. The full 'uns went on one side, on to the catch, I pulled the lever down and it released the tubs and brought them out. The full ones went in to replace the empties. The onsetter was at the full side. The man in charge of the pit-bottom was Mr Diggle. I did this for a while and moved to another job. Where the tubs came out of the cage, ran round, the empties had to coupled up and they went underneath a gantry and onto the main haulage road. My job was then to couple the tubs together. The coal came off the main haulage rope into the pit-bottom, fourteen to twenty tubs on one run. When they got to the pit-bottom the [run of tubs] tubs were split into half, they went down each side, to feed the chair, one to the right and one to the left.

I can just remember the 1936 disaster but I was not working in the *Lidget seam* where the explosion took place and it happened on the night shift. I was on days. I got to know straight away. I went to the pit and my brother, Lawrence, went down the pit as a rescuer. There were crowds of people on the pit-top. The rescue men had equipment on their backs. There were

Fred Elliott, second from the right, outside Wharncliffe Woodmoor 1,2&3 Colliery, c.1962. His mates are, left to right, Ken Jones, Keith Jones and Brian Summerfield. Brian played football for Halifax Town. Author's collection

Fred Elliott with his late wife, Agnes, at the Yorkshire (now National) Mining Museum, Caphouse Colliery, Overton, Wakefield, 1989. The author

ambulances. It was fenced off. I knew some of the men from Carlton who were killed but had not worked with them. We never stopped going in to work. I remember the safety men bringing the bodies out. They had been taken to the low landing and the bodies were brought out the back way and taken into the old school. One man was brought out alive but he died afterwards.

I was then moved into the *Beamshaw* which was a wet seam. It was about a yard or so high. I was working on the pumps. There were a lot of them because of the amount of water. From there I was moved to repairing the pumps and doing jobs with them. I had to go round the pumps, some in the shaft, some in the *Woodmoor, Winter* and *Beamshaw* [seams]. There were centrifugal pumps, ram pumps. My job was to make sure they were all OK. That's where I started to learn my fitting trade. From there I was moved to three regular shifts, days, afternoons and nights, working on the faces and anywhere in the colliery, working on the [coal-cutting] machines, the gear heads, belts, everything and anywhere. The machines were Geoffrey Diamonds and there were others called Mather and Colson, also Samson, only fifteen inches high. The Ace machine was also introduced. I had my arm broken when I was straining a plate on a conveyor belt. Once I was near where a 2,000 volt cable exploded."

(15) Jack Parkin

Born: 12 February 1919
Place: Cronkhill Views, Carlton, Barnsley
Pits: Monkton (No.5); Wharncliffe Woodmoor 1,2 & 3; Wharncliffe Woodmoor 4 & 5; Barnsley Main; Barrow
Mining experience: c.1934–36; 1945–79 (c.35 years)
Age at interview: 85

Apart from army service and a brief spell in lodgings when he worked 'on the railways', Jack Parkin has lived in the mining village of Carlton all his life. It was lovely interviewing Jack and meeting his Hartlepool-born wife, Eva, as I remember the Parkins, as neighbours, from when I was a child in the early 1950s. When Jack left school, in 1932, getting a job was very difficult because of the depressed state of the economy and the mining industry in particular. In this extract he describes, with great feeling and a lot of humour, his early pitwork and also reflects back to his childhood during the 1926 strike when the village was 'bloody destitute.' We

'I'm Proud to be a Mining Lad': according to the commemorative plate held by Jack Parkin in his Carlton, near Barnsley, home, 30 April 2005. The author

also hear about two tragic accidents, the terrible Wharncliffe Woodmoor disaster of 1936, and about some of Jack's very varied later mining experiences.

"It was a terrible day for this community."

"I can remember the 1926 strike. One phrase sums the village up at the time: bloody destitute. Your grandmother would run to the pawnshop at Royston with some of your grandad's clothes, to buy some snap to feed the kids. That was just an example. Everyone was the same. We went to the Sunday school soup kitchen.

When I left school at fourteen to get a job in the village it was next door to begging. I went to see Mr Haigh at Woodmoor and was told that there was nothing doing today, come back tomorrow. I eventually got set on as a kid at Monckton Number 5 [at Royston, about two miles away] as there were no vacancies here. I just went with a pony driver until snap time and then was given a pony to drive into two banks. Then tragedy struck. We had a meeting in the Palace [cinema] and it was decided that Monckton would become 'Laik District' – work a week and 'laik' a week as there was not enough demand for the coal. This would save them keep sending us home after half a shift, what was called 'locked-in'. At some places they called it 'flushed'. We only worked five days in a fortnight. Me and another lad, Frank, decided that we could not live on this wage. At the wall by Brown's farm in Carlton we met Bernard Spinks who asked us why we had no work and told us that he could get us a job on the railway but it would mean going into lodgings in Leeds. It was six shillings a day's pay, thirty-six bob less one shilling and three pence stoppages. It was better than starvation as I was only earning 2s 11d a shift pony driving but for only five days a fortnight. We worked in Leeds and also Bridlington and York and when the war started I was in the army.

I can remember the Wharncliffe Woodmoor disaster [6 August 1936, 58 fatalities]. A woman with a baby in a pram, Rose Hirst, was passing and I said to her that it was a bad day for the club trip to Scarborough. She said, 'Jack, come here lad.' I asked her what was the matter and she told me that the pit had gone off [exploded]. I asked her if it was the *Lidget*. It was. Her husband was one of the men killed. I walked there straight away but you could not get in the pit yard. You would think that Barnsley were playing Arsenal, there were that many people

A photograph from the Royston studio of J L Wood showing Jack Parkin (left) and his younger brother Edwin, c.1919. Jack Parkin

Daily Herald
No. 6390   * *   FRIDAY, AUGUST 7, 1936   ONE PENNY

ALL HOPE FOR 57 PIT VICTIMS ABANDONED

German P For Spa Rebe

AFTER THEIR ORDEAL—Dr. T. F. Quigley, of Cudworth, and Dr. J. Henderson, of Royston, photographed on their return from the workings, and (left) the anxious crowd waiting at the pithead.

SECRET CARGO FRENCH CA

From Our Own Corr

PARIS, Thursday.

NEWS reached French Ministerial circles to-night that a German steamer is now on its way to Spain with a cargo of 28 bombing planes aboard.

The vessel is the Usaramo, which left Hamburg on July 31. Pilots and mechanics for the planes are on board.

The news created a sensation and was the subject of imme-diate informal discussion between Cabinet Ministers and political personalities of the Left.

It is known that before leaving for the south, the steamer called at Emden and completed its cargo with bombs for aeroplanes, shells and machine-gun ammunition.

It leaked out from the members of the crew that the steamer's destina-tion was Spain, but they did not know exactly what harbour.

AT AN END

Even the strongest supporters of the "neutrality" idea begin to admit that things cannot go on any longer in this way.

The attitude hitherto adopted by France has been that of the professional diplomats of the Quai d'Orsay.

It is now openly challenged by French trade union quarters, and was described to me to-night by a spet

BODIES FOUND: GRIM EARCH GOES ON: ONLY ONE MAN SAVED

. hope for the 57 men trapped y the huge explosion in the t seam of Wharncliffe Wood-Colliery, Carlton, near Barnsley h Yorks), has been abandoned.

ly one man came out of the pit alive.

Thirty-two bodies have been found and brought to the surface. A grim, silent pil-grimage of death, they were taken through a crowd of a thousand at the pithead to a church schoolroom, where 40 nurses from a ten-miles area are helping the doctors.

And in that crowd were hundreds of

SORROWING CROWD JOINS IN PRAYERS

Headlines from the Daily Herald, *Friday 7 August 1936, in respect of the terrible Wharncliffe Woodmoor disaster that devasted the community and neighbourhood of Carlton.* Author's collection

there. It had gone up about half-past two in the morning. It was a terrible, wet day. Parson King [Vicar of Carlton] said it was in mourning for what had happened. Parson King was running around comforting people and my old school was used for the bodies, but they were covered up, you could not see them. Rescue teams were there. My Uncle, Lewis Hall, did all the undertaking and when they were burying them the next week it was so hot by the post office corner that the tar on the road was melting under the horses' feet. It was a terrible day for this community. I knew a lot of those that were killed.

After the war I went to see Mr Oldroyd [under-manager at Wharncliffe Woodmoor 1,2 & 3] and he told be to start the next day. I started on the haulage, then went on to the coalface, filling and did all sorts of jobs. When I was 'coaling' the worst job was in the *Low Haigh Moor seam*. It was only eighteen inch. You got the coal the best way you could. When I got home it looked as though a polar bear had been scratching my back. It was terrible. It was cut and blown first. We used short props and if they were too long we made a hole in the floor or had to saw them.

One day I helped a deputy to work out measurements which should have been in linear not cubic. He could not do it so I showed him. When he went out of the pit with the book, on a Friday, Oldroyd asked who had worked it out and the deputy told him that it was me. Oldroyd suggested that went to the night school to be a deputy. I had thought about it but was unsure. Me and Harry Bolton decided to go to night school. I passed, top of the class. At first I had about eighteen months on nights, getting used to the procedures and I finished up with the top deputy's job, in charge of all the developments. I have been told that I was able to handle men. The men worked well under me and I was respected. If there was any difficulty, off came my shirt and I was working with them. My army experience [in the quartermaster's store] may have helped as I was always good at doing figures faster than horses can trot.

I remember, in October 1962, when Don Reed from Grays Road got his back broken. I was with my son, Don, who was my button man and errand boy for the big-hitters. The manager was on the phone asking for me. The accident was on 6's but I said that there was a deputy already there so I should not shove my nose in but I was told to go as I was a good ambulance man. I went there, jumping on the belt which was not really allowed. We got him out of the face and on to the stretcher. He had no sensation in his legs.The lads carried him on the stretcher and I told them that I would catch them up and phoned to say that an ambulance was needed at the Low Deck as I feel sure he has broken his back. He was taken to Beckett Hospital [Barnsley] and then to the Northern General [Sheffield]. The worst job I had was being told to go and tell his wife about the accident. I knocked on the door and Peggy [Don's wife] asked me what had happened. I told her that he was badly hurt and in hospital. She was expecting at the time. The next day I said I would never be dropped on for that job again. I also remember the day that Stan Radford died [when working underground]. His mates chalked a big cross on the wall. Someone put 'S.R.' I showed the inspectors where it happened.

After Wharncliffe Woodmoor closed [1966] I moved to New Carlton [Wharncliffe Woodmoor 4&5] for four years until it closed [in 1970]. It was different, a fresh start. I was then sent as a deputy in charge of the re-opening of Barnsley Main. It was private contractors which was a different outlook. Before the day-wage system came in you had to work out the pay with the team but at Barnsley Main, the measurement of all the work done that week had to be recorded and handed to the manager. Moneywise, I never encountered it, all the work had to be put individually, how much powder had been used, how many dets [detonators] and what work was done. The first job was taking the shaft down to deeper levels, ready for Barrow pit to couple into it. Conditions were OK, though a bit dusty and smokey. It was only fan ventilation, so before the men started their boss would go down with me and check the gas and I did that again at snap time and at finishing time. I was at Barnsley Main until 1974. I had had enough of the hard graft there and moved on to Barrow and stayed there until 1979.

Can I think of any superstitions? My Uncle, Tom Tait, would wash his back on a Saturday. He only wanted to work regular nights, no shifts. He got his back washed on Saturday mornings, that's all. He thought it would weaken his back. He used a hessian sacks, opened out and clean. He would use them to rub his back.

For my leisure interests I used to keep fancy pigeons, called tipplers and some fan-tails. I also had an allotment, growing plenty of vegetables and I was treasurer at Carlton Working Men's Club for seventeen years."

(16) Arthur Morris

Born: 6 June 1919
Place: Worsbrough Bridge, Barnsley
Pits: Barrow; Houghton Main/Wombwell Main; Cortonwood; Rockingham
Mining experience: c.1933–1979 (c.45 years)
Age at interview: 85

Arthur Morris's family are proud of his achievements and attitude to life, overcoming a great deal of adversity over the years. Charles William Morris, Arthur's father, was a trammer at Barrow Colliery when Arthur was born. He can remember him coming home at the start of the 1926 strike, placing his tools in the doorway and saying, 'That's it for a while.' Arthur's mother, Amelia, had died when he was just thirteen and there was a large family to support. In this extract Arthur describes his first day at Barrow pit and work with an awkward pony. We also hear about his widening mining experience, including hand-filling and, unexpectedly, receiving his call-up papers. After the war Arthur worked at Cortonwood, qualified as a deputy and spent more than thirty years at Rockingham, 'the best pit' that he had worked at, prior to ill-health retirement in 1979.

Arthur Morris was happy to allow me to interview him in his Worsbrough Bridge home, assisted by his daughter, Maureen Wood, 12 February 2004. The author

"If your lamp went out … you can't imagine how dark it might be …"

"I finished school on the Friday when I was fourteen and I was straight down Barrow pit on the Monday. My Dad had made arrangements, getting me a job from Mr Dunford, the overman. I got up at dawn, set off when the twenty to five buzzer started blowing and walked to the pit. I went to the office window and told them who I was and was given number twelve check, 'PD' [*Parkgate* day lad]. I fetched my oil lamp, was searched for matches and went down in the cage, feeling elated. All the other lads had taken the ponies, apart from Creamy. There was no training whatsoever. There were gears like chains and a [limmer] bar which used to touch the horse's legs. The bar was hooked on to a tub. As soon as the chains touched the horse's legs he would kick into the air and was really mad. I used to cry, it was so upsetting. I took Creamy along the roadways to the face. I was in the lowgate, fetching the tubs for the colliers to fill. Creamy would only pull one tub at a time. If you put two on she would not move! Martin Schofield, the stableman, told me that I had been left with the worst horse. One day Creamy got away, kicked the props out and was buried but they got him out and he was no worse (or any better!) for the experience. I stuck it out for several months and had experience with other horses. One of them was called Nigger, a lovely little pony. He would do as he was told. If your lamp went out – and this happened to me once – you can't imagine how dark it could be, but I held on to the pony's tail and it took me to the pit-bottom.

I then started working with machinery, on the button, driving the conveyor belts. There was more dust there than when you were working on the face! You weren't allowed to ride on the belts but I did. One day I went over the top of the chute and on to the next belt. That was the funniest thing that ever happened to me.

After that I went hand filling. Picks and shovels were used. You got underneath as far as you could, spragged it and got the coal to drop, then it was shovel and fill. It was a shilling a tub. The seam was only eighteen inches, in the *Parkgate*. I was laid on my side, just wearing shorts, as you were sweating so much once you started working. The shift was from six in the morning until two in the afternoon with a twenty minute break. You can't imagine how cruel we must have been treated. There were about six of us working together. You got paid for as much as you had done. I was hand-filling for about two years."

A young Arthur Morris in army uniform but on leave, Arthur Street, Worsbrough Bridge c.1940. Arthur Morris

Arthur Morris as a young man, Haverlands Lane, Worsbrough Bridge. Arthur Morris

In 1938 we flitted to Brampton and I soon got a job at Cortonwood Colliery, ripping. Cortonwood was a lot better for me as I was more or less working for myself. I was fit as a fiddle, a big strong lad.

In August 1940 I got married to Barbara (we had sixty-two years together) but, in November, I was put on the dole for a fortnight while a drift was being sunk from the *Parkgate* to the *Silkstone* but while I was off, I got my call-up papers. I had to do what I was told! I was half inch too short for the Guards so went in the Infantry, and was sent to Richmond, for the Green Howards. I cried for several nights. After the war I had to return to Cortonwood.

I got talking to my father-in-law and he said, 'Why don't you come with us?' His lot were 'drifters'. They took me to Wombwell Main but we could not get a contract to suit us. I went from there to Houghton Main but we still could not get a job.

My father-in-law suggested that I should go to school to be a deputy. I took his advice and went to sign on, doing my training at Barnsley Mining College in the evenings. After so long I took my test and passed, getting my First Aid and shot-firing papers. I then went shot-firing at Cortonwood, with Roy Yates.

(17) Sidney Cutts

Born: 23 October 1919
Place: West Street, Mexborough
Pit: Manvers Main
Mining experience: c.1933–1984 (51 years)
Age at interview: 84

Sidney Cutts spent all his working life at Manvers Main, starting within two days of leaving Dollcliffe Road School, Mexborough, at the age of fourteen, in 1933. His memories of his early work, particularly pony driving, are shown below, as is his memory of the horrific accident of 4 March 1945 when five Manvers men lost their lives in an explosion. By his mid-twenties Sidney was working as a deputy [and later as an overman], a role in which he commanded the respect of his team of men who he saw as mates rather than subordinates. Quietly spoken but very knowledgeable, it was a great pleasure to listen to a variety of anecdotes from Sid, told with warmth and humour, particularly when he talked about former work friends and colleagues.

Veteran Manvers miner Sidney Cutts with his deputy's lamp and brass memento, in the conservatory of his Mexborough home, 26 March 2003. The author

"I worked out that I had crawled 3,000 miles ..."

"I finished school [Dollcliffe Road] on the Friday and said to my mother, like a big soft kid, 'I'm going to enjoy not going to school'; then my big brother said, 'Sunday neet, tha going down't pit wi me and I've told gaffa.' I told him that I had only just left school. 'Tha'll be alreight', he said, 'as I'm on regular neets.'

I can remember my first night at the pit. Me and my brother walked to the pit [Manvers]. We got to the old baths and from there we went to the Barnsley [No 1] shaft. I was still dressed like a school kid, in short trousers. They gave me an oil lamp. When we got down an overman told me to go to the stables and get a pony and said that my brother would tell me where to go. I went with two more lads who were already working at the pit. When we got there the horsekeeper said 'What's tha want?' I said, 'I don't know. I've been sent here to get a pony.' He fetched me a pony and I asked him how I would put these things [harnesses etc] on him. He said, 'Listen! I'll put them on to-neet but if tha comes to me tomorrow neet I'll give me the biggest clout tha's ivver had.' I could have cried. One of the ponies was Sam, a white horse, and the other was called Charlie. When we got out of the stable one of the lads said, 'Reight, get on its back.' I said, 'What for?' He said, 'To ride on!' It was about a quarter of a mile to travel. We weren't supposed to ride them. Anyway, all of us set off but you had to ride a bit sideways on its back, leaning over as the roof was low. We always did this. When we got there, there was a broken bar, there were no steel arches then, they got under but I forgot to duck and it caught me at the back of the neck. I was just wearing a cap. We stopped at the headings where my brother was waiting and he showed me what to do with the horse. When the tub was filled it was hung on and we took it back, one full tub at a time as it was a steep incline. I managed OK without any incidents until two shifts later. A tub had been filled and taken out of the heading and lowered back down the low side of the heading. I had already done two but on the third that I was loading I could not stop it so I tried with my hand but a bone on my arm was shoved right through towards my wrist. It was my first accident. I was off work ten months. I was only fourteen. There was no compensation. I also lost the tip of my right forefinger, on the face, when I was pony driving, putting a chain on … when the horse got frightened and shot away.

I had two nice ponies, Charlie and Sam. When I left to go into the *Meltonfield seam* I missed them so much that I asked if I could take them home. I used to leave them at the top of the gate and walk down to the workings to check that everything was ready, then just shout and they would make their own way to me. When they were put down I cried like a big soft kid.

When I was at the top of the slit, where the empties came on the rope and then we used to knock them off and send them down to the bottom. Bill Woodall was my mate. He was a bugger for singing and worked further down from me. He sang, 'When I'm calling you', and I would answer with, '… oooh, oooh'. Alan [a deputy], in the box hole, had had enough one day, came out and yelled at Bill 'Thee! I'll put thee an' Woodall in't furthest place in't pit,' and to me he said, 'Thee, Cutty, tha goin back up yonder. I'm bloody fed up of hearing *When I'm calling you!*'

We had to quieten ourselves down. Bill got killed later on.

I was at home when I heard about the explosion [in the *Meltonfield seam*]. They wanted volunteers, so me and Joe [Toft] went to the pit. There was nothing we could do but when we got halfway along the district … we got news that three [dead miners] were being brought up. The first … his eyes, nose and mouth were full of dirt. The second … followed, about a hundred yards behind. His head was swollen and his eyes full of dirt. Another hundred yards and the third one reached us. We were told not to look at him … I knew them all. We started searching for Charlie Leeman but it was a couple of weeks before he was found. A man shovelling on a belt … found him underneath. He had been driving the belt at the level end.

When I shot-fired with Joe Toft we went on a face, 120 yards on both sides, so there were three shot-firers, each with ten men, one at each end and one in the middle. The men liked to

Sidney Cutts checks a shearer cutting run on a mechanised coalface at Manvers Colliery. Sidney Cutts/NCB

get filled off and get out quick but we had set up a good system. The only trouble was the amount of crawling. You had to crawl 300 yards three times a shift, on your hands and knees. I worked out that I had crawled 3,000 miles in my mining life!

I witnessed many accidents when I was a deputy because when someone got hurt I was called for … there were some really bad ones. One young chap was killed on the face … he'd been sat down and had not noticed the roof coming down and was buried with his head on his knees. You almost got hardened to it.

Deputying was a lot of responsibility. I was only in my twenties [when I started] and was soft as a boat with the men. Some deputies would be bullies but I let the men know that I was one of them, not one of the upper crust. I would help if someone was behind … give them a hand, especially the old 'uns. Later, I became an overman. I was well-liked by the men as I did not believe in pushing them. If I saw someone getting a bit extra or a bit less then I would sort it out, just like my overman friend Joe Hartley [qv] who was one of the best. We looked after about three districts and helped each other. We had to see the manager after each shift. I would sooner have worked with the men.

We [officials] had a rough time going to the pit to examine things during the strike but we had to check on safety. We refused to do anything else. Ninety-nine per cent of the men were great, just like brothers."

(18) George Kemp

Born: 24 October 1920
Place: Winn Street, Barnsley
Pits: Wharncliffe Woodmoor 1,2 & 3 ('Old Carlton'); Woolley; Wentworth Silkstone ('Levitt Hagg'); Rockingham; Barnsley Main
Mining Experience: 1934–1983 (49 years)
Age at interview: 83

George Kemp in his New Lodge, Barnsley home, 7 November 2003. The author

I was introduced George Kemp by his son, Peter, who I first met at a family history fair. In recent years George has been virtually housebound, suffering from the kind of respiratory disease associated with working in dusty mining conditions. Despite his breathlessness, George responded to my questions very well. He was born in that old working class area of Barnsley often known as 'Barebones', one of the nine children of Richard and Lisa Kemp (nee Crossland). Richard was a miner all his life, working at Barnsley Main in the hand-got era. In the following extracts George mentions some of his experiences at Old Carlton (Wharncliffe Woodmoor 1,2 &3) colliery, including his recollections of the 1936 disaster. We also hear about his move to Woolley Colliery where he progressed to coalface-work and where he remembered a young Arthur Scargill. A fourteen-year stint at Wentworth Silkstone followed, qualifying as a deputy. The latter part of George's work was concerned with passing on his knowledge and skills to young miners, initially at Rockingham Colliery and ultimately at the Barnsley Main Training Centre.

"The pit had gone up in the night."

"I attended Agnes Road Schools, Infants and Juniors and left in 1934 when I was fourteen … on the Friday and on the following Saturday morning I went to Old Carlton pit for a job and started work on the Monday morning. It was Mr Gothard who I saw there. He asked me where I lived and one thing and another. I couldn't afford any proper trousers so I was in short trousers. On the first [working] day I got some old long trousers to go to the pit in. It was 4 o'clock when I got up. I had to walk from Winn Street into Barnsley and then I caught a bus to Carlton which cost five (old) pence return fare. Sometimes I would walk it to the pit to save money.

I was working on the screens. It was dark and dusty, cold and damp, and also noisy. I worked alongside other boys and an old miner who used to keep us young lads in check. He used to chew tobacco, and was a grand old man. We worked on the shaker pans. Coal was tipped up and the shaker pans riddled the coal, small went on one belt and there were about three belts

69

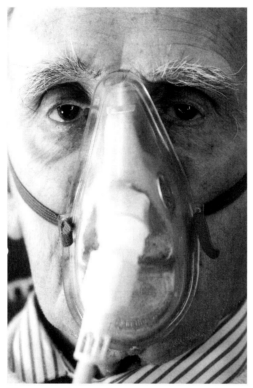

Photograph of George Kemp taken by the Barnsley Chronicle *in 2003 in order to highlight 'foot-dragging' by the DTi in compensating elderly former miners.*
Barnsley Chronicle

for different sized coal. We picked all the dross out and chucked it behind us. I started work at 6 am, we had our snap at 10 am and it was 1.30 pm when we finished. We were paid in cash, half a crown a day.

There was a terrible disaster at the pit [6 August 1936, 58 fatalities]. I went on the bus from town and it was a bad morning, with mist and rain and when I got to the pit there were a lot of people there. The pit had gone up in the night. One of the bosses at the pit-top just said, 'Get your checks, just to show you've been here in the morning and go and sit in the engine room.' There were people all over the pit-top, dashing about. I went to the ambulance room where the doctor was treating the injured. The Union man, Eli Sumnall … was present. Rescue workers were down the pit when we got there. I saw one or two casualties being brought out. They were dead miners. I didn't know them. There were three different seams, the *Lidget*, the *Kent's Thick* and *Low Haigh Moor*, so you did not know everyone. We sat there in the engine room as it was cold, damp and rainy outside, in the loco sheds where there were fires, until snap time and then about twelve o'clock we were told we could go home if we wanted, hand our checks in and catch the bus … back to Winn Street. We did not know what to think when we were sat waiting. I was only a lad of fifteen. I went to work the next day and carried on working on the screens. There weren't a lot of coal turned out that day because a lot of men did not turn up for work because if a miner got killed his mates did not go to work the next day, out of respect.

After working on the screens at Old Carlton for about twelve months I moved to Woolley Colliery. Instead of getting about twelve bob a week you got sixteen shillings working down the pit. Yorkshire Traction ['paddy'] buses ran to Woolley, over the top of Kingstone, picking men up on Park Road. I went down the pit straight away. It was a double-decker cage. I had an oil lamp and later an electric lamp which weighed about 7 lbs and wore old clothes and a belt. I worked on the pit-bottom, shoving empty tubs which came off the cage on this level to go on the main ropes to go to the Silkstone. Later on, I went out into the workings and did some rope running, putting empties on the level and sending them out full of coal.

I remember Arthur Scargill when he was a young lad [at Woolley]. He became the Union man. He was alright. On Friday, if you were tuppence short in your money off your note and you didn't know why, he would help you to sort it. The office might say they would pay it back the next week, but he would insist they sort it out now as you had worked for it this week.

George Kemp (aged 32) enjoying a family holiday in Blackpool c.1952. Kemp family

Elijah Benn was the Union man at that time who, by example, showed Arthur Scargill trade union ways.

I would sneak into the face to the colliers and help them, learning how to go on. I progressed to become a collier when I was nineteen. The *Silkstone seam* was about two foot six inches to two foot eight inches in height. There was the maingate and full tubs used to go off with the haulage and there were two tailgates. Fresh air went through the main roadway and divided between the two gates. Faces were 200 yards long and ten men worked up at the topside of the maingate and ten at the low side. You worked on your knees. Getting to your work place, you each had ten yards of coal, about fourteen tons to shift. This was a stint. You carried an oil lamp, and later an electric one, also a pick, shovel and hammer. You got rid of the gummings so that it would be higher to work in. The face was prepared for us on the previous shift by the shot-firers. A nog-end was placed under the coal to keep it up. For pay, everything was booked down by the chargehand. By ten o'clock [snap time] you felt buggered but three or four slices of bread and fat would revive you. We did not usually leave the face, though we sometimes took five minutes to go into the tailgate to have a stretch. Going to the toilet? Well, you used to have to do it where you were, shovel it into the gob and cover it with coal. You could not do anything else. Some might do it on a shovel and put it on the belt but this was not fair on the lads working on the screens!

George Kemp when he was a mining instructor, Barnsley Main Colliery, aged 58, in 1978. Kemp family

Instructor George Kemp with a trainee at Grimethorpe Colliery, 1980. Kemp family

I decided to move to Wentworth Silkstone pit which was a day-hole [drift mine] at Hood Green in 1947. I'd heard you could earn a bob or two more, so I went there with my mate. I could get there OK as I had a car. I did not booze, gamble or smoke, and occasionally worked weekends, so had saved enough money to buy a Ford Prefect. The two main seams were the *Flockton* and *Fenton* – the *Parkgate* had just about been worked out. It was known as the Happy Pit, as it was a small, friendly mine. I worked there for fourteen years. I started going to the mining college and obtained my deputy's papers and First Aid ticket but never used them, as I was satisfied working with the men.

In 1970, I moved to Rockingham Colliery and worked on a training face with young men, hand-getting and shearing coalfaces, ripping and packing.

George Kemp, instructor (first left), with a group of seven trainees, Newmillerdam Colliery, 1980. Kemp family

In 1974, I got to know from a notice at Rockingham Colliery that they were wanting instructors at Barnsley Main Training Centre. I saw the union man, Sam Illingsworth, who told me that since I was a regular worker and had the right qualifications, I would be just what the NCB needed. I started in 1975. Men and lads needed training. It was a mixture of classroom theory and practical work. We took five trainees at a time down Grimethorpe pit where there was a worked-out seam which served as a training gallery. They could be shown how to use a pick and shovel, boring tackle and so on. Sometimes the pit manager might need a job doing on the surface. I was an instructor there for seven years. I was nearly sixty-three-years-old when I finished in 1983 due to breathlessness, after almost fifty years in coalmining."

III

Born 1921-30

`ANOTHER FULL `UN`.

(19) Frederick [William] Hiscock

Born: 2 July 1921
Place: Stratton St Margaret, Wiltshire
Pit: Wentworth Silkstone (Levitt Hagg)
Mining experience: 1950–1969 (19 years)
Age at interview: 82

Former Wentworth Silkstone deputy Fred Hiscock in the garden of his Millhouse Green home, 17 October 2003. The author

I interviewed Fred Hiscock at his bungalow which he shared with his wife, Beatrice, at Millhouse Green, near Penistone. Fred's first job was as a gardener and groom on a Wiltshire estate. He also had experience of farmwork until service with the RAF, starting in 1940. After the war Fred and his new, Darton-born wife, moved to Silkstone where he worked as a self-employed window cleaner. His trade dropped when he tried to increase his charges by a halfpenny so he decided to apply for a job at the pit, a drift mine, known locally as Levitt Hagg. He describes how he was set on straight away, cleaning the pit-head baths, but he soon graduated and adapted well to underground work, becoming a deputy and overman. Concerned over the uncertain future of Wentworth Silkstone [which eventually closed in 1978], Fred and Beatrice moved to Surrey in 1969, looking after a police residential block, returning to South Yorkshire in 1999.

"We kneeled and sometimes worked on our sides, using a pick and a shovel."

"I went to enquire at Wentworth Silkstone (Levitt Hagg) one morning and I was asked to start work the same evening! It was 1950. First of all I worked in the [new] pit baths, scrubbing and cleaning. Mr White was in charge of the pit-top. He was the engineer. I got on all right with him until I said that I wanted to go down the pit. I think he had me groomed as a pit-top boss but I did not fancy that. I wanted to go down the pit for experience as I had heard people talking about it and it was the best place to earn more money.

Going underground the first time was a real experience and I wondered where I would finish up. I was filling coal. The machine cut the coal out, we put the automatic props up and shovelled the coal on to the conveyor belts. I think it was the *Whinmoor seam* which was only eighteen to about twenty-four inch high. We kneeled and sometimes worked on our sides, using a pick and a shovel. I worked with a team of men. We worked well together. There was usually a ten yard stint to fill off.

I also had a spell boring on the coalface. There was always plenty of dust about.

Eventually, I progressed to shot-firing, after training at Barnsley Mining College. Safety was very important. I had forty 'dets' [detonators] for firing during my shift. I plugged one of the

Fred Hiscock, seen here third right, attended a training scheme at Wharncliffe Silkstone Colliery, Pilley.
Fred Hiscock

Instructors and trainees at the NCB No.5 Area Training Centre, Wentworth Silkstone Colliery. Fred Hiscock is standing, on the extreme right of the group. Fred Hiscock

packets of powder in the detonator, coupled up, stood back and fired. Everything worked all right. I did some shot-firing at the nearby 'Bull & Chain' pit which was eventually connected to Wentworth Silkstone.

I was then asked to be a deputy. It involved a lot of battles. The men were always trying to get more out of me, wanting me to put work down that had not been done. I did not give in. It may have caused ill-feeling but generally we got on well. When the face was started, a set number of men were allocated and you kept this team for the life of the face.

I worked days and afters. I had to be at work earlier than the men. The first task was setting the men on at the pit-bottom, and then walking with them to the face. I monitored things for the rest of the shift. You had to make sure that the supplies were flowing, otherwise the men would just sit there waiting.

One day when I was a deputy I was sat with the overman with our backs to the gob when a fall of rock came down on my back, trapping me with my battery. He managed to get me out, using a pick. That was my only accident.

For my last few years I worked as an overman, responsible for districts which might mean a couple of faces and also checking on men working at any headings. It was all right but if anything went wrong you were the man who took the can."

(20) Stanley Potter

Born: 16 September 1922
Place: Aldham Bridge, Wombwell
Pits: Woolley; Guyder Bottom (Hoyland Swaine); Darton Hall; North Gawber; Woolley; Hartley Bank; Haigh; Woolley; Hazelrigg (Northumberland); Ferrymoor (Grimethorpe); Bullcliffe Wood (West Bretton); Woolley; Old Carlton (Wharncliffe Woodmoor, 1,2&3); Bullcliffe Wood
Mining experience: c.1937–1982 (45 years)
Age at interview: 83

Stan Potter (right) with his friend David Flack at Hay Royd Colliery, Clayton West, West Yorkshire, 5 May 2004. The author

I met Stan Potter at the revived Yorkshire Miners' Gala, held in Locke Park, Barnsley, on 1 May 2004. His wife, Veda, had recently passed away but he told me that he would be pleased to meet me and talk about his mining life. I got a pleasant surprise when, for our first meeting, he had arranged a visit to Hay Royd, a small working colliery at Clayton West which had been in the ownership of the Flack family for several generations. Stan's enthusiasm for mining history was infectious. As a young man he moved from pit to pit, usually drawn by the prospect of slightly better pay or to get away from bad working conditions. He was the only miner that I have interviewed who worked using a candle for light, in a small drift mine called Guyder Bottom at Hoyland Swaine. After his marriage he settled down to a thirty-five year stint at Bullcliffe Wood, West Bretton, retiring due to occupational ill health (respiratory problems and a back injury) in 1982. In the following extracts Stan describes his remarkable experiences as a young trammer and summarises his later employment which even included a short spell in Northumberland.

"Here's your candle lad ..."

"By the time I was turning fifteen ... I thought that if I could get at Woolley [Stan had worked for about a year in two woollen mills at Clayton West] I could get 17s 6d a week. Father was not keen and you always did what your father said but he eventually allowed me to go. At Woolley, on my first day, I was terrified when I went down the shaft in the chair. It was a double-decker one. You held on to the handrails and down it went – whoosh! I was set on tramming tubs round into the cage and did other jobs too.

Tramming was very hard work along low roadways as can be seen in this early, c.1900, photograph, an example from North-East England that Stan Potter would empathise with. Notice the lad's candle is placed on a lip near the bottom of the tub, near his left hand.. 'Trammer's scab', a bruised and cut back, was an understandable occupational hazard of this job. Shorts or 'tramming drawers' were sometimes worn.
Author's collection

I was at Woolley until just before my sixteenth birthday when a chap was visiting next door asked me if I wanted a tramming job at a pit at Hoyland Swaine called Guyder Bottom, a day-hole [drift mine] owned by, I think, a Mr Marsh. It was five bob [shillings] a day which I thought was a fortune! I soon found out what tramming really was like. First he [the collier Stan was working for] told me to get some clay out of the bankside near the pit entrance and to keep working it with my hands, like plasticine, spitting on it and getting it going. Then he said, 'Here's your candle lad.' The colliers had to buy their own candles. We went down and into the pass-by and he uncoupled a tub and started tramming it, to show me what to do. The candle was stuck in the clay and placed on the tub. On the Main Level, about 5 foot high, it was OK but when it came to going up the Low [Gate] it was only a yard high and fairly steep. He pushed it up OK and told me how to drop it off at the end of the rails, leaving a little gap to throw coal into the tub. When the tub was filled he just put a locker in the back wheel, lifted it on the rail and pushed and slid it along, from the back of it. It looked easy to do. He then said, 'Reight, you take that tub back.' Well, it did not work so well for me. I could not push the tub like he did. I tried using my head against it as I hadn't enough strength in my arms and had not his balance or technique; then when it came to coming out with the tub I had not got the knack of going over the sleepers. My clogs hit them and my back kept hitting the roof. When I got to the end of the gate my back was streaming with blood, all along the vertebrae. I wore a pair of clogs, a pair of tramming drawers [long-legged pants] and I was stripped to the waist, just wearing a cloth cap. My father worked seven days a week on a farm and got twenty-eight shillings but I was earning thirty bob for six days. It was big money for a kid. Later, I was in the kitchen getting washed and mother came to wash my back and noticed all the torn flesh. She said, 'Oh Stanley, what a mess. You can't go there again.' I told her that I had to go as I had told my father that I could do the job. Young pride! I stuck it and got used to keeping my back down and trammed like he did.

Then I got chance to work with another collier for six bob a day so I went with him, at the same pit. Colliers could compete with each other for better trammers. I finished up tramming for seven bob a day, for Sandy Senior. He used to take his full pillar of coal out but then ripped at one end to make another crossgate higher up, so he could afford to pay me more brass. Sandy bought me an acetylene cap lamp which was grand, lovely under the Low but in the higher gates I used to run and jump on the tub, to have a ride, facing the air but the flame, six to seven inches long, would turn towards you and singe your eyebrows!

If your carbide went out and you were short of liquid you pickled [urinated] in it – but it used to stink horrible! Sandy had an accident, slipping on a flagsheet and broke his leg so I had to find someone else to take me on, maybe for less brass, so I decided to leave.

I went to Darton Hall Colliery which worked the *Low Haigh seam*. It was a shaft pit, but only about a hundred yards deep. I was twisting on the flagsheet, pushing tubs under the loader. I got good pay there, nine bob a day. It was warm conditions and hard work, you were at it all the time.

Then I got a chance to earn £1 a day on the coal-cutting machines at North Gawber. It was a gassy pit and hot, deeper than the others. I was in the *Lidget seam* which was only 2 foot 6 inches but reasonably comfortable. I was kneeling all the time, using a shovel at the back of the machine, moving the muck into the gob behind me.

I then went back to Woolley, in the *Silkstone seam*. I was filling for a while. There were over 2,500 men there. I also did a bit of coal-cutting, on the machines, shifting the muck and then left. Something did not suit so I was prepared to move.

I moved to Hartley Bank, between Netherton and Horbury Bridge, working in the *Flockton Thin seam* which was just 1 foot 6 inches high. You were laid on your belly and side. It was machine cut though but I worked mostly on development.

I then went to Haigh, working in the *Beamshaw* on the cutting machines. It was a wet and damp pit, with a bad roof, a poor pit to work at, another day-hole.

I went back to Woolley, in the *Parkgate seam* but from there went up to Northumberland. I just wanted a change, drew my life savings of £12 out of the bank and went to the railway station and asked where the next main line train was going. It was to Newcastle, so I booked a single. I had no idea what I was going to do. Pits did not come into it. I went to Hazelrigg Colliery at Wideopen, near Gosforth, and worked there as a market man.

I returned home after about six months, maybe a bit homesick but had difficulty in getting a job until I got set on at Ferrymoor in Grimethorpe Colliery yard, working in the *Shafton bed* but I found it too far to travel. I had to set off at 3. 30 am on days, to walk to Barnsley, to catch a bus.

In August 1947 I got a job a job at Bullcliffe Wood, near West Bretton. It was a day-hole, with about 200 men, working the *Top Haigh seam*. I did six months on the coal-cutters but left in June 1948 as it was a wet pit. It was about this time that I met Veda, my future wife, on a bike ride to Holmfirth. We married in 1949.

I returned to Bullcliffe after a six month gap when I tried millwork again and short spells at Woolley – in the *Blocking seam* – and Old Carlton. When I returned to Bullcliffe it said 'Not wanted' by my name but the overman gave me another chance. I stayed there until 1982, my longest spell at any pit. Wilf Hartley was the boss. I settled down there after I was married. I was filling in the *Barnsley seam*. One Christmas eve I got a big stone on my leg when I was using an air pick, and was off work about six to seven weeks. I worked regular afternoons for a long time on contract. I got so much a yard for coal-cutting. Some deputies may have referred to me as a hot-headed bugger and I did sometimes fly off the handle but others handled me better. I was never a yes man. Dennis Bowden, the under-manager, used to ask me what sort of temper as I was today before asking me to do a job.

I decided to take early retirement in September 1982, aged sixty, on health grounds as I had had a back injury two years earlier when I braced myself to drag a pulley out from under the conveyor belt. I had been taken off face-work due to dust on my lungs.

Stan Potter (right) with his mate, Dick Adams, still doing a bit of tramming in Bullcliffe Colliery woodyard, c.1980. Stan Potter

Stan Potter recharging his old pit battery in the lamproom at Hay Royd Colliery, Clayton West, West Yorkshire, 5 May 2003. The author

I have had forty-five years employment in coalmining and continue to take an interest, as a hobby, taking photographs and videos and visiting Hay Royd Colliery at Clayton West, thanks to the owner, David Flack.

The best thing about mining life? Well it was pay day! and the worst thing was the accidents."

(21) Norman Rennison

Born: 11 November 1922
Place: Grimethorpe Street, South Elmsall
Pit: Frickley
Mining experience: c.1937–1982 (45 years)
Age at interview: 81

Norman Rennison at the pulley wheel dedicated to the workforce of Frickley/South Elmsall collieries, 5 November 2003. The author

My interview with Norman Rennison contained some detailed information about pony driving and most of his comments are included here. Norman spent his entire working life at Frickley Colliery, where his father, John, also worked as a collier. Getting set on, however, was not easy since pit jobs were then scarce and his relatively small size did not impress. After pony driving Norman progressed to haulage work and then, about the time of his marriage and when the butty system was still in operation, to contracting. He was made redundant in 1982, aged almost sixty.

> *"... it was dangerous as the roof was not very high,
> so you had to lay on them,* [the ponies] *riding in the dark."*

"I went to see the under-manager, Mr Kay, and kept begging for a job and he kept telling me, 'Come back when you are a bit bigger'. Eventually he gave way. On my first day it was not easy getting up so early. Mother put my snap up. I went for my checks from the office, one to go down and one to come out with, also a metal pay check. It was a steam-powered winding engine. The cage was a single decker with about forty men in it. It was held for a few minutes and then it went whoosh, half a mile down. Your stomach went into your mouth!

I had a heavy electric lamp hanging from my belt but sometimes you took an oil lamp, depending on the job. It was rare to notice any gas. I worked in the pit-bottom for a few weeks, to get used to things, getting empties off the chair. I wore a pair of old trousers, a black beret on my head.

I did some pony driving. Your number was on the board and I was told to get a pony out. An old bloke called Tom Scott was the ostler. There were different sorts of ponies. At South Kirkby they were more like cart horses compared to ours which were more like New Forest ponies. I drove one which was called Gypsy. It had its tail trimmed, a lovely little pony but it got killed, though not by me. The bloke was taking him out, through the doors, but he should not have taken him through before he made sure that anything was coming, so it was hit by some tubs and was put down. They used a spiked cap for this, the shape of the horse's head, with a hole in the middle and a spike went in the hole and was banged with a hammer. We used to have to fetch dead ponies off the units on trams which were like tubs with no sides. I rode the ponies but would have got the sack if I got caught. It meant that you got to the pit-bottom quicker but it was dangerous as the roof was not very high so you had to lay on them, riding in the dark. It's surprising how the ponies kept their feet because of sleepers and holes and

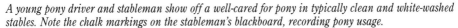

A young pony driver and stableman show off a well-cared for pony in typically clean and white-washed stables. Note the chalk markings on the stableman's blackboard, recording pony usage.

that. You must not hang your coat up with an apple in your pocket anywhere near a horse as it would eat it. Once I took my pony into a tub stall, in a one-way system, when a pile of muck fell on the tub and a shovel was needed to dig him out but someone hit him and I played bloody hell. The pony struggled and finished up on top of the tub which was full of muck and it was a hell of job to get him off. At holiday times we took the ponies out of the pit and into the fields. A box, fixed with wooden sides, was used to contain them on the chair and was wound up slowly but it was a job getting them out because of the metal plates that the tubs slid on, as they slipped on them. Sometimes I had two ponies, one in a sling gear, with straps and a chain to hang on to a tub and one with limmers, steel shafts put on the pony. Sometimes you needed two ponies because there was so much weight to pull.

When the war started [1939] tins of beans and fruit were stocked in the stables. You were supposed to brush your horse down. I used straw for this and its coat used to come up shining. The ponies got to know you. Some were Welsh Mountain ponies and a few were Shetlands but they were really too small. One was called Dot, a great little worker. Another was called Pride, a grey, who used to bang his collar at the back of the tubs and would shove 'em with his collar, near a hundred tubs at a time but they were small, not like the big modern tubs. The ostler would keep the stables clean. There were mice but he had a couple of cats and they got a bottle of milk every day."

(22) Frank Johnson

Born: 25 December 1922
Place: Carr Lane, South Kirkby
Pits: South Kirkby; South Elmsall
Work: 1936 to 1982 (46 years)
Age at interview: 80

Enoch and Myra Johnson, Frank's parents, had thirteen children, their two-bedroomed terrace in Carr Lane described by Frank as 'a bit crowded.' Derbyshire-born Enoch worked at South Kirkby Colliery. Myra came from Staffordshire. I always enjoy meeting Frank and his friends on occasional Saturday afternoons in the Empire Working Men's Club, Moorthorpe. He was kind enough to let me interview him at his South Kirkby home. Married to Molly, they have recently celebrated their diamond wedding anniversary. Frank recalled his early days at South Kirkby Colliery where he worked from 1937 to 1942, finishing forty years later at South Elmsall/Frickley where he worked on the faces and on headings.

Frank Johnson in the garden of his South Kirkby home, 5 August 2003. The author

"I was so small I could not look onto a Barnsley bed tub!"

Frank Johnson with his wife, Molly, September 1985. Frank Johnson

"I left school in 1936 when I was fourteen and for about a month attended Doncaster Technical College. I asked my brother to get me a job at South Kirkby Colliery as he worked there. I had to be down the pit for six in the morning, so was up at five. Mother would get up with us. I started work in short trousers and my first job was in the pit-bottom, coupling tubs on. I used to lift the link up and put my thumb under the hook and couple them on. There was a cage full of us when I went down. I was so small I could not look into a *Barnsley bed* tub! As the tubs came down and they started winding coal, coal ones went down one side and empties down the other. You had to twist 'em and shove them through drop chairs and I used to couple them on. When you had about twenty tubs you would lash 'em on and send them up and someone would be waiting to take them out of the pit-bottom. The *Barnsley bed* was a warm area, so conditions weren't too bad. The first wage that I drew at South Kirkby, for six shifts, was 19s 11d.

I did this work for several months until I was sent down the roadways to do some pony driving. Each driver was responsible for the pony that he took out. I would go to the pit-bottom stables first to rig the pony with its harness, ready to fit the limmers. I would link the limmers on to the tubs by dropping a pin down and you set off but when you came to an incline there was another horse with chains on, a trace horse which you could used to help pull. I can remember some of the horses' names. There was Harrier, Pablo…. Some would work their hearts out and others, well, you had a job to make them go. The Landing End stables were about half a mile further underground from the pit-bottom stables, providing ponies for working in districts further underground. I remember one occasion when a pony was 'britching', like heading back at the tub … The rails were fishplated together and it must have got its back foot fast and its hoof was ripped off. I had to report it and the horsekeeper who came from the pit-bottom and put a cap on the horse's head. A spike was fitted to the cap and this went into the animal's brain when hit with a hammer. I got to know the ponies and took them sweets and apples, and bits of snap. I was about twenty when I finished pony driving.

There was an industrial dispute I remember at South Kirkby in about 1938. On a Friday afternoon some of the lads got together and started emptying their dudleys. It was a nice day and they were not going to work. I went home with the majority but I didn't know why there was a problem. The pit stood idle and no work was done. We were fined as it was private enterprise and we had to go to Pontefract to pay the fine [ten shillings/50p] in court.

I moved to South Elmsall Colliery in 1942. It was a new pit though it had been opened before and headed out and then closed but it opened up just before the war and was associated with Frickley Colliery. It was still under private enterprise. Things were very strict and you could be fined. I started on the haulage and then went on machines. The ABC Arc Waller was a machine on wheels. We had to flit from one heading to another to cut the coal. As face-workers we had six yards and one foot for each of us. there would be about twenty men on a face, throwing the coal onto a belt. When you had room for a bar you would set it. Each man would

Frickley/South Elmsall Colliery in the mid 1980s, shortly after Frank Johnson retired, when, according to the NCB, three seams were worked: Cudworth, Top Haigh Moor *and* Dunsil. *The* Meltonfield seam *was also under development. The CEGB, via Ferrybridge 'C' and Eggborough power stations, took most of the coal. The two pits had functioned as a single unit since 1968 until closure in November 1993.* Author's collection

set five to six bars a stint. I did some ripping as well. Ripping meant that if you were in an advance face there were two gates, you must have an intake and an outake for air and as you advanced there was the maingate rip and the tailgate rip and you have to keep up in the roadway and set arches or rings. The turnover was five foot. We would have a belt and stinting you would turn over five foot and you would put packs on at each side.

There were no pit-head baths when I first started work at South Kirkby so I had to come home in my pit muck, so the copper had to be heated for water and we had a tin bath. I didn't use the canteen much, I was always early arriving in a morning and the last away so as to miss the crush in the baths.

For my snap I used to have dripping and a bottle of water. We had twenty minutes and just sat down anywhere. We used to crack jokes, even a bit of singing. There was always some banter when the belt broke down. There would be so many working on the belt and some would get it mended but the others might be listening to a character talking and joking in his stint, passing time on.

I was fifty-nine when I finished, on 16 January 1982. I was in hospital later the same month with a brain tumour. I remember my last day at work. I was making junctions. I couldn't wait to finish! I've enjoyed my leisure time, apart from the year when I was ill. I always enjoy going to the Empire Working Men's Club and have a pint of Tetley.

In my younger days I played football for Carr Lane and South Elmsall Juniors, South Kirkby Colliery and played a bit of cricket.

Best thing about nationalisation in 1947 was that everyone got the same rates of pay.

I was retired when the 1984 strike started. Thatcher intended getting the miners down as I think she drafted soldiers into the police force against the pickets. I thought Arthur Scargill was a good bloke.

Conditions in mining were very bad and I have seen a lot of miners who died young due to the conditions. When chocks and mechanisation was introduced conditions did improve, it was more comfortable work. I am totally deaf on one ear, which may be due to the sound from the machines."

(23) Frank Beverley

Born: 19 June 1923
Place: Upper Sykes Street, Kingstone, Barnsley
Pits: Dodworth, Darfield Main, Woolley, Haigh (day-hole), Carlton (Wharncliffe Woodmoor 4&5), Redbrook (Dodworth), Rob Royd (Dodworth), Dodworth
Mining experience: 1937–1984 (47 years)
Age at interview: 81

Frank Beverley's family are proud of his mining achievements, and rightly so. I was introduced to him by his son, Tony. It was immediately apparent that Frank's first-hand knowledge of the industry was considerable, based on almost half a century of work at Barnsley area pits. His father, William Beverley, and three brothers, were also miners. Frank never aspired to become a deputy but combined pit work with voluntary work on a Kingstone Farm, often working extremely long hours. Towards the end of his mining employment Frank worked as a water development engineer, though he was occasionally diverted to a variety of

Frank Beverley was still able to demonstrate his 'coaling' techniques when I visited him at his Worsbrough Dale home on 15 December 2004. The author

underground jobs, including coal-filling and laying rails. In his retirement, and not surprisingly given the conditions in which he worked, he suffered from respiratory problems and, sadly, died shortly after this interview, in January 2005.

"Little Man, You've had a Busy Day."

Frank Beverley, ready to leave school, and start his long stint in the coalmining industry, starting at the screens at Dodworth Colliery in 1937. Tony Beverley

Young miner Frank Beverley enjoys a walk at the seaside. Tony Beverley

"I went to Dodworth Colliery and got a job in the screens at ten bob a week. The manager was Mr Spedding, who was a nice chap and lived in the pit grounds, in a bungalow. He sent me to see Mr Sellers who was in charge at the pit-top. Being young and not right strong, you would sometimes nod off to sleep but the boss was stood on a gantry above us, throwing bits of coal to wake us up and shouting 'Come on!' I don't think he wanted to come into where we were as you could not see the lad next to you. I was moved to another department where the bigger coal was – and bigger pieces of muck! Later on, I progressed to another conveyor, but there was a lot of dust again. This was where the coal and the dirt were bound together so we had to throw them and split the coal from the dirt with a tool called a nadge, a pick with a hammer head. One of us had to sweep up, to keep the dust down. I always remember when it was my turn they always sang *Little Man, You've had a Busy Day.*

When I got to about fifteen I applied to go down [the mine]. I used to think that you went down the cage you could see all the men working, in different levels. I had no idea! My job at the pit-bottom was on the haulage. Timber came down the shaft and I had to couple them [the tubs] and use lashing-on chains. One lad would put the front chain on and another lad [would] put the back chain on. There was a run of sixteen tubs but we had no idea what the workings were like. It was bitter cold. Sometimes, we huddled in a man-hole, a place dug out of the side, enabling you to get in if any transport accident happened. I wore old ordinary clothes, just a cap on my head and clogs on my feet. You got fed up of doing the job. It was so cold.

When I worked on the screens and on the haulage we had 'tipple tin day'. At Friday you went to this window, where there was a little bob hole, and you put your hand in. On the shelves inside there were little tins with money in and this bloke might say, 'Tally number 1322' and get 1322 tin and tipple it into your hand. It was ten shillings a week which I gave my Mum. Then it rose to 12s 6d and Mum gave me 2s 6d back.

Eventually I moved further from the pit-bottom and went onto the levels, where the tubs went up to the coalface. Then I got on to the faces. We took timber up to the face. We had a dragger, a rope, which we put on our shoulder to drag the trams [containing timber] up to the coalface and then we emptied them. It was heavy work. There were also arched rings that we lifted. We dragged them up the gate, for the rippers, when they were advancing.

There was no chance of getting a job filling coal. Two or three of us decided to go buttying, working for a bloke who would get the money and who would then pay you. You could be working in a team of men, say four, and two might be getting more money than you, doing the same work. There was a chargeman on the faces and he got what was called the big note, and he would divide the money between us, in the pit yard.

When I went with this bloke [called Ashurst] there was me and my mate and another mate and their three Dads. It helped us get away from Dodworth. We started working at Darfield Main [but] were not there long, modernising the pit-bottom, but he paid us little money. We were young and wanted to enjoy life, so when we were on the afternoon shift there was a gate called Windy Nook with bent girders. The air came from Mitchell Main, so if we wanted an afternoon off we nipped up Windy Nook, turned the air valve halfway, went back into the headings where we were working, start our jiggers up but they were not doing anything, no power, so we sent for the deputy, saying there was no power. The pipes were rotton from Mitchell's to Darfield, so the manager was called and he would tell us to go onto the pit-top, empty a couple of wagons and then we could go. But we only drew a 'Bevin' for that day. If we had been working for a measure we would have got more money. When we were advancing, we had girders for the roof support and there were big oil drums there but one day the machine caught the drum when we were in the heading, widening the plane. I was with the deputy, stemming for the shots. All the girders came down. A bloke grabbed me and, luckily, it was a rock roof and no dirt came down, otherwise we would have been buried. We just got the skin off our backs.

From Carlton I went to the staple pit at Redbrook. A shaft was being made from below ground in an uphill direction. There were wooden boxes in the staple pit, one in each bay, and there were bars across. I had to climb up these to get to the top. You never knew what to expect when you went up and it was worth a shift's pay to go up just one. An Irishman and the deputy were going up at the start of the shift and got so far up this box when the Irishman collapsed, squashed the deputy and killed him. I had to replace the Irish bloke. It was not a nice job.

I went to see the manager at Dodworth, Mr Ramsey, and asked him if he could find me a job. He said it was awkward as Ashurst's men were working for him at Redbrook. I did not want to go back to Redbrook. He said he would find me a job [at Robroyd] on the haulage. I wanted to progress but I had just got married and needed the money, so I accepted. I lived at Worsbrough, in lodgings, and biked it but it was too far for me to go from Rob Royd to Dodworth to the baths, so I went home in my dirt. The tin bath fitted in the pantry and that's where I bathed! It was a nice pit. The deputy, Alf Winter, saw me in the pit-bottom and said, 'Hey up, want a job? Start on my face tomorrow and get some tools.' I had never worked on a face. I got some tools from the Dodworth stores and the blacksmith stamped my check number, 1322, on the blades of the pick and the hammer. I had to pay for them. One of the deputy's men, 'Mint' Harris, had gone into the headings, to earn more money, so there was a vacancy. It was in the Low Gate where there were teams of five. When you had done your stint and you had made everything right you could finish early. But I had not noticed the chalk mark on the roof but got to know. I had been leaving too much for my mate. We would chalk our marks and we would help each other out. When we had filled off and timbered up the deputy gave us a note to go out of the pit. Then I moved to the *Thorncliffe seam*. If there was no work on then I was put on the haulage again. One day I was working in the pit-bottom and the deputy asked me to take some blankets down to the workings as there had been an accident. I set off running and when I got there the stretcher party came through the air doors and this bloke had a white handkerchief over his face, he was dead. He had been dragging rings with a rope up to the face when he collapsed. That gave me a shock. The *Thorncliffe* was about three-foot high. Then I worked in the two-foot *Flockton seam*. I had to lay down on my side with a shovel and pick and my mate, Carl, would dig holes for his knees and he would stay there as long as he could reach. We used little props with a lid, sometimes steel bars. You had to shuffle backwards. I wore knee pads. I got used to it, you had to. You just got on with your job. I wore a helmet with a lamp. We called them Shuttle Eye caps like the ones that they had at that pit. I got knocked out once when I was drawing off and I caught the last prop. The man that had set it had not put any wood at the top. I was unconscious and carried out."

(24) Roy Kilner

Born: 8 December 1923
Place: Prospect Road, Bolton-upon-Dearne
Pit: Barnburgh Main
Mining experience: 1937–1983 (46 years)
Age at interview: 80

Roy Kilner is the fourth (of five) children from the marriage of George and Margaret 'Daisy' Kilner (née Lunness). George Kilner worked at Hickleton Main, initially underground, and then on the pit-top, where he maintained and laid rails for the coal wagons. Roy attended infant and junior schools in Bolton-upon-Dearne and the new Dearnside Secondary, leaving at the age of fourteen to work at Barnburgh Main, in December 1937. The following extracts are based on an interview recorded at Dearne Valley Venture, Bolton-upon-Dearne. Roy remembered composing and singing a little song on his way to the pit on his first day, his experiences as a young miner, and

Roy Kilner at the commemorative pulley wheel marking the site of Barnburgh Colliery, 3 September 2003. The author

his progression to becoming a fitter. Latterly, following an accident in which he suffered a back injury, Roy worked on the pit-top, before being made redundant in 1983.

"... I'll be off to Barnburgh Main on Monday morning"

"The last week of December me and a friend went to Barnburgh pit to get a job. We went into the under-manager's office and enquired, 'Any vacancies, Sir?' and he said 'Does any of your family work here ?' so I said 'Yes, my uncle Ted Lunnes'. 'Oh', he said, 'He's a good worker. You start on Monday'. We collected our hard hats and our pit boots from the stores and then as we were going home we made up this little song [sings]:

> *With my snap tin on my belt*
> *and my dudley on my bike*
> *I'll be off to Barnburgh Main on Monday morning.*
> *With my hard hat on my head*
> *and my pit boots on my feet,*
> *we'll be off to Barnburgh Main in the morning!*

On my first working day I was up at half-past four in the morning. Mum would be up with me as she always got up with dad, to cook his breakfast. She made my breakfast and put my snap up. Jam was very acceptable, or dripping, or cut up tomatoes. Things had a different taste down the mine. You could even eat sour apples or grapefruit. I walked about two and a half miles from home to the pit, over the railway bridge and down the lane but when I arrived – I was wearing shorts – I went to the lamp room because the baths were there but I had not been given a bath place. When I did get one it was a rope with several hooks on, and that was where I hung my pit clothes. You put your pit clothes on the floor, got a shower and then put your night clothes on, put your pit clothes on the hooks and pulled them towards the roof. I got a bucket lamp but when I had my arms straight down it dangled on the floor! so I had to carry it with my arm bent. I was so small that I could not look over the tubs.

Let me tell you about the first drop. It was a terrifying experience because everybody got on, there were twenty men on the cage, but I was so small I could not reach the bar to hold on, so held on to a hole on the cage. Everyone told me I would be OK. Then you dropped, about 500 yards, but slowed up as you reached the bottom and your tummy settled down. I got off the chair and someone took me and told me to leave my snap and lamp as it was all lit up at the bottom. We left them in a cubby hole.

My first job was chain dragging. Chains were very essential in the pit, hung on to the tubs, about five or ten at a time and then placed on to a rope with with five or six laps and hooked on to the hook. One had a hook on and one had a ring on. My job was to take them off – as they came up full of coal. The man who took the chains off would throw them on top of the coal and my job was to drag them through to the other side of the shaft where I would throw them into empty tubs. As the coal went into the chair it was carried to the surface and run off into skips and the other chair would come down with empties on. I had to keep them chains going. There were two of us and on the lower deck. There would be another boy taking them off the lower deck and throwing them on to the top deck for me and my mate to pull them through the shaft. The top deck wasn't too bad as regards lowering the chains but on the bottom deck it sloped and there would be men there with lockers, putting them in, and had to move fast, sorting them before getting to the pit-bottom. I did this for about four months and then cleaned lockers. There were devices for greasing the axles of the tubs and my job was to take the grease off the lockers so that the boys who were putting the lockers in did not get it on their hands. I did this with stone dust.

There was a bad accident down the *Parkgate* in 1942. It was terrifying to see tubs stuck in the roof. On my first job there I had to go and see the under-manager for a week, asking if a job was available, eventually getting a job as a pony driver. I was frightened to death as the pony was so much bigger than me. I remember some their names – Jedda and little George. They could be temperamental but they knew what the job was and carried on doing it. I used take them apples and carrots. Once in the stables the horse-keeper, a man called Green, gave me a horse called Jolly. He told me to go in Jedda's stable and take a bucket a water. I got in OK but, when I clanked the bucket, the horse jumped up and lashed out. I fell and said that I was not taking him. But he told me that it was my horse for the day!

There were a lot of mice in the pit, so you had to watch where you put your sandwiches which was why it was a good idea to have a proper snap tin. Mum used to pack a small one for me, with a close-fitting lid, and it could be hung on my belt. Those who took it in snap paper or loaf wrapping paper could hang it up but the mice would climb up and find it.

I finished pony driving when they had just started a new face and my job was to slap tickets on tubs. You had a roll of letters and I had to lick the gum and stick them on the tubs but after so long I thought of an idea, involving the use of a tin with water in and a piece of sponge which could be fastened to my belt. This saved me from the nasty taste which was terrible. I did this for about two years while the face was being worked and then went to another district, the South District, and eventually went to the pit-bottom and uncoupled tubs as they came out through the skip. Barnburgh was a skip-winding pit.

I was asked about face training. I went pan-turning in 1947. My job was to turn the pans over. As the coal was taken out we would advance the pans and they had to be taken to pieces so as to slide them to the next run where it was built up again. I had a bit of trouble with Fred, the trainer. We went out early, as instructed, but had two bob stopped. I went to see about it and the under-manager said we had gone out early but I told him that Fred had said it was OK as we had done our job. He asked me if I was happy in the job and I told him 'no'. I was told to go back to my old job of uncoupling tubs. After a month or two I enquired from the foreman fitter if I could go fitting and so I trained to be a fitter and did that job from 1948 until redundancy in 1983.

I worked seven days a week, even before being a fitter. Sunday work made things easier for mum and dad. I married in 1946. Before I only got £1 a week pocket money from a £3–4 wage.

Roy and Sarah Ellen Kilner after their marriage at St Peter's Church, Edlington, Doncaster, 10 June 1946. Roy Kilner

Barnburgh Main worked the Meltonfield seam in the mid-1980s, the coal sent to the nearby Manvers plant for processing. NCB/Author's collection

I got injured in 1970 and started working on the surface but it was still a hard job, repairing chocks, despite my bad back. Then I had another accident in 1979 when I was repairing a motor. The crane driver asked me to carry on while he went to the toilet. He left the chains on. I carried on but someone jumped into the crane cab, we did not notice, and started it up, putting it into gear but it jumped and a hundred weight motor landed on me. We had got it on pieces of wood, it slid off and hit me on the groin. I stood up but fell down again.

I enjoyed my life in mining as Barnburgh was a happy pit because of the colleagues that I worked with. I never needed to go anywhere else. I had some great years and, for me, it was a pleasure to go there.**"**

Roy Kilner by a concrete plug over one of the principal shafts at Barnburgh Main.
The author

(25) George Hurst

Born: 25 September 1924
Place: Bolton-upon-Dearne
Pits: Barnburgh Main; Goldthorpe; Wath Main;
Manvers Main; Wath Main
Mining experience: 1938–1983 (45 years)
Age at interview: 79

George William Hurst has lived all his life in the village. One of four children, George's father, also called George William (b.1901) moved to Bolton from Mansfield (where he had worked at Park Colliery from the age of thirteen) in about 1915, finding work at Banburgh Main; and later at Brodsworth and Wath Main. In this extract, from a conversation recorded at Dearne Valley Venture, George recalls his life in mining, from starting at the screens at Barnburgh – where he had to work at the pit or face possible imprisonment – to 'deputying' at Wath Main.

Former Wath Main deputy George Hurst, Bolton-upon-Dearne, 29 September 2003. The author

"I decided I did not want to be in jail, so went down the pit."

"I was fourteen when I left school in 1938. I could not get a job so spent six months at what we called the 'Dole' school at Mexborough. At the time I was an altar boy at the church and the vicar wrote to several places and gave me references but I couldn't get an apprenticeship. They were setting lads on at Barnburgh Main and Dad told me that I could go to the pit but had only to work on the pit-top. I started on No.6 screens. It was dusty and noisy but was swept up after every shift but I would not have worked on No 5 screens for a pension! I worked on the screens until I was seventeen and a half years old [1941] when I had to register for the armed forces. I was called into the manager's office, Paine they called him, and he told me that I had to go down the pit. I said that I did not want to but I was then told I would be sent to jail for six months and would have to go down the pit afterwards. I decided I did not want to be in jail so went down the pit. At the time they started bringing Bevin Boys in as they were so short of men.

My first job was as a pony driver. I was told to go and get so and so pony and had to go to the stables and get a pony and go down the district. I was dealing with loaded tubs and taking empties to tub stalls. There was Old Sam and Bonnie. When Old Sam was retired a bloke bought him for ten bob and kept him for a pet at the end of Green Lane, in a house. He was a good horse. Some of the ponies knew when they had more than two tubs on. They would not move! They could hear you putting the links on.

I always had bread and dripping for my snap and perhaps on one day bread and jam. Mother put my snap up. When I first started work, on the first day, Dad got up with me and cooked bacon and egg and tomato and he told me that this was the first time and the last! I had to get up on my own from then on. I used to walk to Barnburgh, over the Station bridge. It took about twenty minutes to half and hour. I used to leave the house at five for a six o'clock start. I was pony driving for about twelve months.

After pony driving I went on haulage work, knocking coal on and lashing on and knocking empties off, doing that job until I was about twenty-two. That's when I went training to go on the coalface. I trained down the *Parkgate seam,* for about three months or six months, packing and drawing off, ripping, pan turning [turning the belt over when the face had been filled off] and coal-cutting. Faces were terrible when I started. There were a lot of weight bumps. On the training face Percy Petty and Harry Royston were my trainers and I can remember when they shouted 'Run!' and there was such a bump and when we went back on the face the coal machine had been blown over into the gob [waste]. The face was six foot. The *Barnsley seam* was five foot six inches. I used a shovel, pick and a hammer for knocking the timber up. We got a day wage when training. I went back on to the *Barnsley bed* when my training had finished. There was eight yards of coal, called a stint, and I had to fill that up. All the men on one face were on one note, they all got the same except the bookman or 'bookie' who used to have about three yards of coal and used to measure the stints out. If somebody had got filled-off he used to tell them to go and help someone else. We earned about thirty-two or thirty-three shillings a day. I did this until I was about twenty-five years old, about a year after getting married.

My father-in-law was deputying at Goldthorpe pit and he suggested that I come to his pit and I would get more money, so I went there, but I was two bob a day worse off! It was known as the 'Sludge' pit because there was a lot of water. I worked on the tub stalls, only eight foot wide. My first wage after I was married was £6. I only stayed at Goldthorpe six months. There were three drifts to go down and one to go up and they stretched under where the motorway [A1(M)] is at Doncaster.

Dad then got me a job at Wath Main in the *Haigh Moor seam.* It was a good pit. I earned about fifty bob [£2.50] a day there, working on the face. When *Haigh Moor* was closed down I moved to the *Meltonfield seam,* dropping to thirty-two bob [£1.60] a day. I finished there and went to Manvers Main but only for six months in what they called the Dips and it was white hot, all you wore were your boots and your belt for your lamp, your helmet, and nowt else.

I returned to Wath Main. I got buried there a time or two. We were on this face and there were six of us with a machine which used to go through … one was at front pulling cable, one of us on the machine and four of us at the back breaking lumps up with a jigger pick and there were two timbering up at the back of us. It used to leave perhaps a foot of coal which came down but I was under it. I remember Bill Roberts, he was a big bloke who said to me, 'I'll get thee out, Jud.' He grabbed my belt and lifted me straight out. I thought he was going to pull me in two but I didn't care as long as he got me out. I just carried on working, I wasn't really hurt. I finished on that face and we were doing a bit of daetelling work, a bit of all sorts, and we were at a junction when a lump of muck came down and hit me on my back. I think I needed twelve or thirteen stitches but the deputy did not want me to go out of the pit. I was taken to hospital, had stitches and penicillin.

I became a deputy and did twenty-one years. It was a big responsibility but if you had a good set of men you were alright. I knew the faces I was on and that I had some good men. When we started with the new machines, Doscos, we went into the headings and faces, there were six in the team and they were the best workers in England. You had no need to bother with

George Hurst outside his former home at Bolton-upon-Dearne, 29 September 2003. The author

them at all. When I went down into the headings they often told me to 'go away' as they were OK. I did not have many disputes, apart from with the under-manager.

I was fifty-nine when I was made redundant. It was the end of July. I had been having chest problems anyway, so went to my doctor but eventually he told me that he had instructions to throw me off sick but he advised me to come back on the Monday and he would place me on the club again. I signed on the dole. I was pleased to finish. I've enjoyed my retirement since then. I had two allotments to attend to. I have enjoyed my working life in mining. I have had some great friends, some good working mates, even when I was on the haulage and I do miss all the humour."

(26) Colin Massingham

Born: 29 January 1925
Place: Victoria Street, Darfield, Barnsley
Pits: Dearne Valley; Darfield Main; Dearne Valley; Houghton Main
Mining experience: c.1939–1985 (c.47 years)
Age at interviews: 75 & 79

Colin Massingham has kept a meticulous record of almost forty-seven years of his mining experiences, which included twenty-eight years working underground. His father started work in 1900 at Darfield Main as a trapper, aged twelve, moving to

Veteran Dearne Valley Colliery miner Colin Massingham in his pit helmet, Wombwell, 23 July 2004. Colin worked at Dearne Valley for almost twenty-eight years. The author

Dearne Valley Colliery twelve years later. Colin's older brother started work at Dearne Valley in 1927. Colin was able to recall, in considerable detail, how he got his first pit job and his early working experiences, starting on the screens as a fourteen-year-old. Underground work began on 10 July 1940, as a stemming lad [making clay pills for the shotfirer). We also hear about a short spell at Darfield Main and vivid accounts of roof falls. He moved to work above ground in 1967, in the offices at Houghton Main, becoming responsible for the home coal arrangements which proved to be a particularly difficult task at the start of the 1984/85 strike, affecting his health. Colin officially retired on 30 September 1985.

"She's going! Switch the machine off!"

"I had left school for three months and could not get a job anywhere. I told my Dad that I would have to go the pit but it was not with his blessing. I was fourteen and three months when my brother turned round and said, 'Come with me tomorrow morning', which was a Saturday, and he took me to see Mr Worthington, manager at Dearne Valley. He took me up to the office door and I stood waiting. I asked how I would know him and my brother told me that he comes down in a blue and grey Morris 14 car. The car arrived and a tall chap, over six foot, very lean, walked forward and I said to him, 'Excuse me Sir. Are you Mr Worthington?' He said, 'Yes, what do you want, lad?' I told him that I had come to see about having a job. I went into his office and he asked me my name. I told him and he said 'Is your father Fred Massingham?' I

Dearne Valley Colliery main haulage adit, photographed by Colin Massingham on 31 August 1963. About 200–240 full tubs per hour were wound out of this drift. A conveyor system replaced tub haulage in 1968.
Colin Massingham

said he was and he also asked me if I had a brother called Leslie. I told him yes. Right, he said, come to the pit on Monday morning, just before six and see the under-manager. Come with some pit clothes on and we will set you on.

Monday morning was May Day, 1 May 1939. The under-manager wasn't present but a boss surveyor, Ernest Hanwell, and his side-kick Bob Gomersall, were there. I was taken to the screens on the pit-top which was my first shift. What a job it was. Steel-moving plates, clanking and banging about, coal flying all over..and the job was to pick all the muck out … stone and brass and stuff. For six days (6am to 2pm), my first week's wage was 18s 11d. We had a twenty minute break … snap time – I took a bottle of tea and stood it by the side of the old steam engine that drove the screens, to keep the tea hot, despite all the grease. Back on to the belts at 10. I stuck it for two or three weeks and saw the pit-top foreman, Bill Hacket, telling him that I could not stand it much longer … the noise was driving me dizzy. He told me he had just the job for me. He had a job for me in the paddy house … making pills for the shot-firers.

I then asked to go underground. My hours were 9 to 5 but at 2 o' clock a youngman who was a motty-shouter (every tub filled, those that filled it had a metal token on some tar band which would be thread through a hole in the tub and on to hook attached to the inside of the tub … when it went back to the surface and weighed the motty shouter gave it to the weighman and there would be a shout, '74….' next tub '1 and a pair of 111's' … 'No 5' … and the weighman always weighed before booking them down. Checkweighing they called it. The

Colin Massingham was still able to demonstrate traditional mining techniques when I visited his Wombwell home on 23 July 2004. The author

men down the pit were paid on what they filled. When I started on the machines, in 1940, it was a shilling or 1s 1d per ton. The tubs held half a ton, so two had to be filled … that was for machine coal but for hand got coal all that came off the pick point … using pick, hammer and wedge … I think that was 2s 2d a ton. On these faces there were just two men, a collier and a trammer, paid on one note, but it was shared between three on machine faces. I was a gummer so I wasn't on the note. As the machine undercut a four foot six inch seam my job was to use one of two rakes to go under the cut and pull all the gummings out or waste sleck. The seam at Dearne Valley was four inch of coal, four inch of dirt [muck band] and four foot six inch or nine inch of coal. The machine would cut out the muck and I had to rake it to the side and shovel it away on to spare land. We did not have a gob in this type of mine so there was spare land for gummings. I spent nearly two years on the machines and then went on Jones' haulage engine which was only ten horse power. Soon the traffic manager [Alma Walker] came and said he wanted me on the slant road and worked on the drift slants … it was a level but it dipped down and went up again at the far end and was 1600 yards long..I was on Ball's Slant (named after William Ball who first started it). When I had got forty full tubs I clipped them onto a rope with a clip at the back … and the weight of the coal would push the tubs and they would all stretch out in a long line; then I put a clip on the front … rang the haulage man with a knife on the overhead wires …

I only had a short spell at Darfield Main, in 1944, for three weeks. I'd heard that the pay was 13s 10d a shift compared with 13s.6d at Dearne Valley. I was set on pony driving. I had never done any before, taking empty tubs down to the face and bringing full tubs back. I felt a bit timid at first going down the cage. It was about 260 yards down to the *Beamshaw*. I went on old 6's face. It was OK when it was all ripped and you could stand up and walk along but down at the face it was a shock … top side of face was two foot six inch and low side just one foot nine. Men worked laid down on their sides with short-handled shovels, It was a heck of a job … not for me.

Roof falls were regular but we always got a warning … one night shift I was sent to into the timber drawers [two men], down Turner's, as my mate had not turned up. It was all worked out, stood on props. I had to go to the far end and pull all the props out … good ones were sent out and used again … so many were taken out and then we would listen and you would hear a creaking, whining noise … so then we would get out of the way … if the top went we would have no chance … it was four foot nine high … come on lads it's warned us … bumping upstairs … we went back as far as we thought would be safe when there was an almighty bang and crash and all the rock came in … hundreds of tons came down..to within ten or fifteen yards of us … it was like a sold wall of rock, impossible to get through to save anything … On another incident, when I was on the machines with my mate, Arnold, we were cutting one place … the machine slicing the coal … I tapped him on the shoulder and shouted 'She's going! Switch the machine off.' We could hear the noise from the roof so I told him we had to get out even though he wanted to finish the cut … two or three lumps of stone dropped..so we moved when there was a big bang and an almighty crash, dust flying all over … We waited a few minutes and went back to look what was left … but the machine was buried by massive rocks.

I got buried partly once [1942] and injured my shoulder and hip when cutting a heading … we didn't think the stone would drop and I was gumming out again when a big lump of coal came on top of me … it caught me on the shoulder and pushed me on to the machine which had a row of jagged teeth … it must have weighed three or four tons and held me down on the machine which was still running. My mate jumped up and switched it off. I remember saying to him 'Get me off it, Eric!' He got hold of it and just eased it. I sat down, held my head in my hands..I was on afternoons … I told the deputy that I was going out of the pit and asked for a note but he said he dare not give me a note even though I showed him my injuries, blood running down my side but he made me stop until the end of the shift! I was seventeen. There were no baths at the pit and the medical centre was just one bloke, so I went home in my pit clothes, got bathed so I could see the damage and went to the Drs the next morning and was off work for two weeks.

Pit baths came to Dearne Valley on 17 November 1951, most of us made use of them. The canteen had been opened in July 1942, a director called Curtis opened it and our first dinner was free, meat and potato pie for me. Previously there was a small corrugated iron hut at the end of the lamp room but all that was sold was Albert Hirst pork pies and little bottles of milk. There was no seating. We just sat down outside, on the floor. I had then to walk almost two miles to get home and bathed.

I enjoyed my pit work. There was not a job at Dearne Valley that I could not lay my hands to.**"**

(27) Joe Hartley

Born: 21 September 1925
Place: Burman Road, Wath-upon-Dearne, Rotherham
Pits: Manvers Main; Askern Main (Bevin Boy training); Darfield Main (Bevin Boy); Manvers Main
Mining experience: c.1939–1983 (44 years)
Age at interview: 78

Former manvers deputy Joe Hartley, Quarry Hill Road, Wath-upon-Dearne, 8 April 2004. The author

After leaving Park Road School at the age of fourteen Joe found work with George Heseltine Smickersgill, a local builder, at a time when air raid shelters were in demand. When his new boss was called up Joe managed to get a job at Manvers, his Dad's [Frederick Hartley's] pit, working on the screens. Joe tried to join the armed forces but opportunity was limited to submarine recruits which he declined, finding work instead as a driver's mate (and then driver) for Yorkshire Farmers. When attempting to volunteer again attention was drawn to Joe's application which included his previous work at Manvers. Remarkably, he was told to report Askern Colliery as a Bevin Boy. The following extracts, based on an interview and Joe's own notes, relate to his Bevin boy training at Askern, his first 'posting' to Darfield Main and subsequent work at Manvers where he became a deputy and overman.

"We had to join up."

"I was shocked when I found out [that I was a Bevin boy]. There were lads from all over the country, including Cockneys. I think we were the third lot to train there, for a four week spell. Fred Hall was the instructor at Manvers and we spent a week underground in the safety school. We had a week underground and were shown [for example] how to put on a locker, how to couple a tub safely and how to gear a horse up for pony driving. At Askern we also did physical training, stripping down to shorts and vests and ran around the countryside and did marching, wearing pit boots. Some of them needed it. I remember the *Bevin Boys' Anthem* which went something like this:

> *We had to join up*
> *We had to join up*
> *We had to join up old Bevin's army*
> *Fifty bob a week*
> *Wife and kids to keep*
> *Hob-nailed boots and blisters on your feet*
> *We had to join up*
> *We had to join up*
> *We had to join old Bevin's army*
> *If it wasn't for war*
> *We'd be where we were before*
> *Old Bevin your barmy!*

A happy scene at the Manvers Main banner, Yorkshire NUM Gala, Barnsley, Saturday 19 June 1965.

I was then sent to Darfield Main but used to pass three pits to get there! I was seventeen and a half years old and the only Bevin boy. Tommy Spooner was the Union Secretary. There were some good lads at Darfield. I worked at the pit-bottom to begin with, by the chair, dealing with full and empty tubs and helped with the haulage. It was very cold in the intake shaft. I wore an old boiler suit that I had used in my lorry driving days. The men treated me OK. Working on the haulage, I remember one lad called Smith who came to work wearing a butcher's smock. He would feed the ponies with pickled onions from his pocket. There were no pit baths, so I came home in my muck. When you travelled on the service bus you got some looks, passengers wanted to keep well away from you.

After about eleven months at Darfield I got transferred back to Manvers, working underground in the *Swallowood seam*. I was put on the tub haulage and then went on to the loader but after a few months was on the face, filling, using a shovel and a pick. I drew my first week's wage on the face at Christmas 1945. Once, I got buried with coal, on the morning shift. They pulled me out but I continued to work and filled off.

I remember the 1945 disaster in the *Meltonfield* but I wasn't working in that area. I heard about the explosion at nine on a Sunday morning. I knew all the men who were killed. It took several days for Charlie Leeman to be found. His dog had been taken down the pit to try and help locate him. He was eventually found on the Thursday. Ernest Corker had cut the belt when it had got fast, and Charlie was found underneath it.

I changed from filling coal to turning pans on the face; and then to boring. I had worked with a man who had done some roof bolting and I was then given the opportunity of attending to a difficult face that kept breaking down, so there was only one way to sort it. That was my in road to further progress. I was encouraged to became a deputy so thought I would give it a go, attending Mexborough Technical College to obtain my ticket. I became an official in 1960.

I was shot-firing for about six months first. There was a change to power-loaders and some men were not interested in it but I took to it OK. I became the face overman and seam overman and progressed to senior overman from 1964. It was a lot of responsibility. By and large I got on well with the men. A deputy needs to be a knowledgeable man, a patient man and a fair man. The hardest thing was when you were supervising men that had been your workmates.

I decided to retire in 1983 when I was fifty-eight, finishing on 8 August. I missed the comradeship and all my friends. During my last week I did not go underground. I was presented with a pair of cut glass decanters. Mining gave me a good living. I experienced some good times and some bad times. I never thought that our coal industry would disappear in my own lifetime."

(28) Dougie Pond

Born: 12 December 1925
Place: Kilnhurst, Rotherham
Pits: Kilnhurst; Barnburgh Main; Kinhurst; Wath Main; Manvers Main
Mining experience: c.1937–1984 (47 years)
Age at interview: 78

Dougie Pond is a well-known character in and around the Wath-upon-Dearne area, partly because of his poetry, often written and recited with great humour and in dialect. Dougie has been a guest on BBC Radio Sheffield and has won awards for his verse. A collection of his poems, *Lookin' at Life Above an' Below Ground in Verse* was published by Dearne Valley Venture Ltd in 1994 and reprinted several times. The following extract concentrate on his early mining experiences, particularly at Kilnhurst Colliery and concludes with Dougie's poem *Words of Poetry*.

"What makes the pit is the men."

"I was born at the back of the Commercial Hotel, Kilnhurst, called Hick's Square but known as Pottery Yard. I had five brothers and two sisters. We lived in a terraced house, one door at the back and one at the front, with just two bedrooms. My dad [Harold] worked at Kilnhurst pit which we called 'Bob's 'Oyle'. Mother [Annie] had all of us to look after and no one could make Yorkshire pudding better than her. She was little and stocky and so was my dad.

Former miner and published poet Dougie Pond, Dearne Valley Venture, Bolton-upon-Dearne, 4 November 2003. The author

I attended Kilnhurst Council School, leaving at fourteen. I said I wanted to work on the pit-top or be a cobbler! My dad took me to see the pit-top gaffer. I was in short trousers and started after Christmas. I remember the foreman, Charlie Cooper, saying to my Dad, 'Whose this massive looking giant?'

On the pit-top I was the motty and errand lad most of the time. The motty on the tub meant that they knew where it had come from. There was a tar band and 'medal' with numbers on. Before they put them on the tipplers it was taken off and thrown down and I had to collect them all together, sort them and put them back on the hooks. I did this for twelve months. My next job was was working with the empties … as they went up the gantry I put hooks on the back so they would not catch when they came off. That was my last job on the pit-top.

It was an experience going down the first time [aged sixteen] but you were with other men and they were talking and laughing. We called it the chair, fifteen on top and fifteen on the bottom [deck].

At Kilnhurst I was getting the empties, hanging 'em on and sending 'em to what we call the loader. They were filled there. I did this for about four years and then went to do face-work. I was on the motors. I got used to it and one of the belt men left … I was the beltman then. It was the *Silkstone* face which could be a yard high but there were places when it was low, so lumps would get fast and rip the belt and break it. Machines cut the coal. It was very dusty. It was hand-filled. There was a lad on motors, my old job, and I was there in case the belt broke. What makes the pit is the men. You could work somewhere with a set of miserable buggers and you would not feel as if you were with men who were always laughing.

I got transferred to Barnburgh and worked there for two years. A lot of Kilnhurst men got moved. There was a bus from Meadow View where I had lived from the age of fourteen.

Dougie and some of his friends and work colleagues photographed underground at Manvers during National Safety Week. On the back row are (left to right) Wilson Davies (deputy), Freddie Lewis and Arnold Dodds (under-manager); in the centre: Bernard Swift, 'Rockin Billy' and Eric Mirfin; and at the front: Gary (?), Jack Kilkenny (manager) and Dougie Pond. Dougie Pond

Barnburgh was the first time I had experience with pit baths as there were none at Kilnhurst. It was OK at Barnburgh.

I returned to Kilnhurst, working again in the *Silkstone* and got married to Iris [nee Hope] in 1950. It meant me cycling from Wath to Kilnhurst and coming home in my pit muck again but I was living with her parents and they had a bath.

I got a job at Wath Main [closer home] but it was very damp there. My snap, in a snap tin, felt soggy! I gave over taking snap and could not settle, only staying there a month.

Harold Mann set people on at Manvers. He told me to see him in two weeks. I moved to Manvers and stayed there over thirty years. I enjoyed Manvers. I was on the loader, and then ripping … when the coal had gone the roadways are made higher to take the tackle through … you took the rip off and set rings or archway. I came out of the faces when machine faces arrived and was put on supplies. They wanted about three times more supplies than when it was hand-filled …

I was fifty-eight when I finished, in 1984, just before the strike started.

I came home from work one day and the wife had been washing the paintwork down and she was blaming 1001 cleaner for her red hands but really she was allergic to copper. My check number at Manvers was 1002. That started me off writing my first poem:

WORDS OF POETRY

'Ere is some words of poetry
About serious side of life, but mo-er on the funny
Thirty years of lookin' black at Manvers Coll'ry
That's weer I use t' earn mi money.

I've worked underground for above forty years
Been a miner awl mi life
We've jus' two sons and one daughter
That's me and Iris mi wife.

I've been asked this question mo-er than once
And many a miner will 'ave' been asked the same
If ever I could live my life o'er
Would I go back int' pit again?

Well I awlus look two ways at this
An' without any shadow of doubt
I'll say "No I wouldn't" when I think of dust, sweat an' toil
Or "Yes I would", when it's the men I'm thinkin' about."

(29) Geoffrey Shone

Born: 5 September 1926
Place: Havelock Street, Low valley, Darfield
Pit: Houghton Main
Mining experience: c.1940–83 (c.42 years)
Age at interview: 77

I met Geoffrey Shone for the first time at Low Valley Methodist Church where he has now been organist for over fifty years. He has also had a long association with Wombwell Mixed Choir and Houghton Main Male Voice Choir. Geoffrey's father, Enoch, was one of the many Staffordshire-born migrants to Low Valley, finding work at Houghton Main in about 1900, retiring at the age of seventy-nine. Geoffrey told me how he got 'set on' at his dad's pit, and sent underground on his first day, conveying

Geoffrey Shone at the organ, Low Valley Methodist Church, 20 November 2004. The author

materials to face-workers in the *Parkgate seam*. After more haulage work and a spell as on the conveyor belts yet more haulage work followed but he was able to progress to 'wireman' status, assisting the electricians. This job was interrupted by a back injury, one of two painful accidents that he experienced. Geoffrey tried working underground again following his back injury but was unable to cope, so was employed in the pit-top electrical shop for twenty years, until retirement in 1983.

"We did not know who or how many had been killed."

"Sammy Bellamy was the under-manager in *Meltonfield* at Houghton Main and prior to leaving school he ran a class on safety measures at the pit. I joined it and he said that lads who finished school could come to see him and he would get them a job. My dad worked there and also my older step brothers. On the Monday morning at six I reported and went down the pit, to the *Parkgate seam*. I felt lost and did not know what to expect. From the pit-bottom I went to the box hole, and they told me that I would be going with 'Doc' Baxter who was in charge of the timber. He had a little goatee beard and he said 'Right we are going on this gate and we got to the coalface and he said 'Right lad, go down the face and see what all the men want'. Well, I did not know what a face was, I didn't know anything at all but the face was pointed out and I was told to go down there and get to know what the men wanted, and write it on a piece of wood, with chalk. So off I went. First man wanted so many props and so many wooden bars and so on, until I got up to the top. One of my jobs was to go down and take these wooden props off the belt or the Panza at the end of the shift. It was really terrible, getting bathed and then home for dinner. It was a case of dropping off to sleep during my dinner. I got paid about £1.2s.6d for five days.

I was in the *Parkgate* for about twelve months and then went into *Meltonfield*. I worked in the pit-bottom for about six months and then went onto the haulage, packing and putting empties on to the road to send them down to the loaders, to the pit-bottom. From there I went on to the face as a tension lad, keeping the belts running free. I did this for four or five years and then went back on the haulage, lashing tubs on to the main road either empties going down or full ones coming up. I then went to the *Beamshaw* after the *Meltonfield* closed down, for six months, then back into the *Parkgate* as a wireman, helping the electricians. I was there until I hurt my back, three slipped disks in my neck and was in hospital on traction three weeks. I was pulling a cable tight when my foot slipped. I was off work nearly twelve months. I'm still suffering with it. I got compensation when I was off, a weekly sum but nothing by today's standards. When I was on the haulage I got my little finger trapped (and eventually taken off) and was off five months and when I started work they gave me six pence per week but they said they had overpaid me so I had to pay them back!

I worked with my oldest brother, Enoch, and his son, Arnold and a team of repair men and at snap time we sit down and we would start singing. One of the favourites was *Cwm Rhonda*, *Guide Me Oh Thou Great Redeemer*. One Christmas we sat down and we sang carols.

I was at the pit when the terrible disaster took place in the *Newhill seam* in 1975 when two of my mates, Ray Copperwheat and Len Baker, were killed. They were in the electric team like me. I was on the surface, working on days and I had come home at the end of my shift and Ray and Len were on the six o'clock night shift. I went to work the next morning but didn't know anything about it and then we were told. There were quite a few injured. We didn't know who or how many had been killed. We were all stunned. There were emergency vehicles and rescue teams in the pit yard. Everybody knew the people who had been injured and killed. One chap was recognised by a Bible that he always carried. They recovered all the men. VIP visitors included Tony Benn MP, Arthur Scargill, the union compensation secretary, Joe Gormley [NUM President] and Derek Ezra [NCB Chairman]. There were TV and newspaper reporters. In the days afterwards the pit closed for a short while until the investigation. We started work as normal as could be. We wanted to attended Len and Ray's funeral at Darfield church but we were not allowed. The boss said that if we attended we would not get paid. We could put a note in for 'lieu' days but we were told if we went to the funeral we would be in breach of contract.

I kept working until 1983. On my last day I emptied my cupboard, at half past one, and clocked off and that was it. No ceremony or presentation."

(30) Kenneth Hammond

Born: 16 March 1927
Place: Third Avenue Upton Beacon, near Pontefract
Pits: Upton; Bullcroft
Mining experience: c.1941–1966 (c.25 years)
Age at interview: 76

Ken Hammond's father, James William, was the winding engine man at Upton Colliery, working twelve-hour shifts, so Ken felt it was 'only natural' for him to get a job at the same pit, especially since he had developed an interest in engines from a young age. In this extract we hear about Ken's experiences as a fitter, beginning as a raw apprentice and progressing to foreman status. Ken also provides us with a useful description of the Upton Colliery site and describes the shaft filling, after the pit closed in the mid-1960s. His next move, to Bullcroft Colliery, did not last long, a pit he regarded as old fashioned compared to Upton. He then found employment as a fitter at Ferrybridge 'B' (and later 'C') power station, retiring aged sixty-three. Like many miners, Ken has had a long and active interest in sport which he also describes in the final extract.

Former Upton Colliery fitter Ken Hammond holds an Oaks Colliery Bible, presented to one of his ancestors following the terrible disaster of 1866. 29 April 2004. The author

"We used to pester the foreman ... to take us down the pit."

"My dad arranged for me to have an interview with the enginewright, Mr Ralph Welford. He worked in a little dingy old office, nearly on the shaft side, reached by three steps down into it. He was sat at a desk with just a desk light on and asked me why I wanted to work in the

Upton Colliery fitting workshop, part of a modern range of service buildings erected for the new colliery c.1930. The timber structure (background, right) was the foreman's office and beyond that, through the opening, was the blacksmith's shop. Ken Hammond

fitting shop. I told him about my interest in engines. and was told to start on the Monday, so I only had two days off school.

During my first few months I spent my time tapping nuts out and screwing bolts. They used to save all the old bolts and put them in bins. As an apprentice I had to screw them and grease them, put nuts back on and put them in the 'done' box. I did that for three months, and became sick of the sight of 'em. I also had to mash up for about thirty men so had to learn about every snap bag, where it was, which was his [each person's pot]. There were some right battles! I got paid £1. 3d. for five eight-hour shifts and a Saturday morning.

I used to take a pop bottle of tea which I hung with string on the blacksmith's bosh to warm it up and if you had time as an apprentice you would toast your bread but we used to sneak our snap in working time and then play cricket and football, or nipsy, at snap time! They were happy days. There were ten apprentices in the fitting shop and goodness knows how Arthur Curry used to put up with us.

Bill Dixon was the main man I worked with. He showed me how to screw-cut and so on. The fitting shop was crude, a wooden floor made of railway sleepers and a bench of the same material, with a great big stove in the corner, four foot six high and two foot six diameter, with a great big home-made kettle on top for mashing up with and a big coal bunker by the side. It was very cold in winter.

An oblique aerial photograph showing the extensive surface buildings at Upton Colliery. Ken Hammond

We used to pester the foreman, Arthur Curry, to take us down the pit and eventually he did but, unknown to us, he had phoned the winding engineman and asked him to give us a rough ride. It was funny to him but not funny to us. We went into the *Winter seam* which was only one foot ten. We did not understand what was happening – we could hear these voices but there was nobody there, so we asked Arthur where the sounds were coming from and he told us to bend down and then we saw the men laid on their backs with great pan shovels. What a job that was.

A colliery is a self-contained unit. There was the boiler plant, steam pumping engines, electric pumping engines, a big power house – since there was compressed air to go down the pit. We had a steam turbine that compressed 16,000 cubic feet a minute and a big reciprocating compressor which came from Grimethorpe Colliery. It was huge, having a seven foot six inch diameter piston. There was a Bellis and Morcom reciprocating compressor, an Alley and Maclean reciprocating compressor and a Browit and Lindley generating plant. There were also pneumatic rams on the shaft side for ramming tubs into the cage and two sets of creepers which picked tubs up from ground level up into the screens; and then there was the washery which had a big bucket elevator on it, taking coal into the washery. There were tipplers for the tubs, three steam locomotives. Upton had one of the deepest shafts in the area, 734 yards and twenty-one foot diameter shafts. At one time 1,200 were employed.

As a fitter, I went down the pit nearly every day. We did not go on the faces but looked after the pit-bottom machinery. It was mainly the ramming-on tackle that went wrong, perhaps when it had blown out of its cylinder, so a new piston was needed. Some fitters were a bit tight, reluctant to pass on their knowledge. I became foreman fitter because of my experience. There were about twelve to fourteen fitters under my responsibility. Winding engine men and power house men were also on my books.

The pit finally closed in 1965 but closure had been discussed for quite a while and the Union had been battling with the Coal Board to keep it open. The explosion that happened was perhaps what they needed to say 'that's it'. It occurred underground. From what I have heard … there had been a gob fire so the ventilating fans had been shut off over the weekend, so the headings had filled with gas, and when the fans were started on the Monday morning the gas went into the gob fire area and up the lot went. Jimmy Petrie, one of the deputies doing the inspection, got killed. At first they could not find him but when they did the blast had blown him under the conveyor … his clothes and everything was missing … it was a very nasty job.

All the foremen were kept on as we had to supervise the shaft was being filled which was quite an experience. The cages were kept on for a while at No 2 shaft and No 1 shaft was being filled, so what happened was that one cage was lowered into the bottom and it was disconnected from the winding rope and the rope was wound on to the drum which left the other cage in the pit-bottom. Then the winding rope was cut and the noise, from the rope coiling got louder and louder so you could hardly hear yourself talk and the earth around was trembling. I'll never forget it. Another incident happened when we were shaft filling – we had a air-driven little hauler with piano wire and a plumb weight on and as they were filling lorry

Upton Colliery Cricket Team, 1945. Back row(L-R): A Wolsey, Richard Taylor, C Smeaton, G Ball (Sec), Ken Hammond, Fred Taylor, S Whitehouse, J Slater; front row: J Manterfield, D Smith, W Dixon, Robert Taylor, J Hill, W Slater, PC Hubbard, A Brown. Ken Hammond

loads of rubbish was put down the shaft, filling it, we would lower the plumb bob down at the end of every shift to see how far it was coming up but it never came up so we had to go down No 2 shaft and in to No 1 bottom to see what was happening. All the strata that we had tipped down had mixed with water, like a molten mass and it was creeping into the south drift so we would never had filled it so we had to start throwing all sorts down then – brick walls, tub sides, to try and consolidate it at the bottom which we eventually did.

I played cricket, football, badminton and table tennis; and later on golf. I now play snooker! As a lad I played nipsy or peggy. We used to grind a slope on a hammer shaft and grind a little flat on the top and cut it off about two and a half inches long. You put it [the peggy or nipsy] on a brick and tapped it with a stick, it would jump up in the air and you would give it one. Two sides played in a challenge match. You might be challenged to sixty jumps or strides. If you thought you could manage it you might try and reach it in fifty-eight and that score was yours; but if you failed that score was his; also when you hit the nipsy up … we all got good at it … you could keep tip it up three or four times and then hit it and that trebled or quadrupled your score. We played as apprentices at so-called snap time."

(31) Edmund 'Ted' Horace Lunness

Born: 17 February 1927.
Place: Furlong Road, Goldthorpe, Barnsley
Pits: Barnburgh; Kilnhurst; Barnburgh; Manvers Main [as Subsititute Manager]; Cortonwood [as Manager];Orgreave/ Dinnington/New Stubbin/Firbeck [as Mining Engineer: Special Duties]; Manvers Main Complex [as General Manager];
Related employment: Rotherham Enterprise Agency [Executive Director]
Mining experience: c.1941–1988 (47 years).
Subsequent employment: Business Consultant
Age at interview: 77

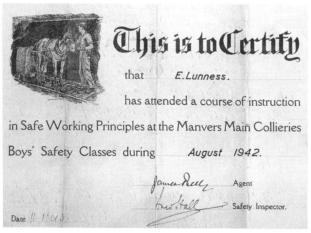

Ted Lunness at his Thrybergh home, showing a certificate presented to him for attending a Boys' Safety Class at Manvers Main in August 1942, and also a First Aid/Safety medal. In the background art-work can be seen from Ted's grandchildren, Kazia and Charlotte Caruana.
The author

Ted Lunness has had a long and impressive career in the mining industry, rising from work as a boy trammer and pony driver at Barnburgh, to a young overman at Kilnhurst; and then back to Barnburgh, as under-manager, a few years later. Still in his twenties, Ted was appointed to the new post of substitute manager, working at Manvers during a major reconstruction phase. Aged thirty, he moved to manage another big pit during a period of modernisation: Cortonwood. Later, as a senior manager, Ted had a roving role, advising at a number of collieries, prior to being appointed as General Manager at the large Manvers complex. In 1985, George Hayes, the NCB Area Director, asked Ted to help establish the Rotherham Enterprise Agency, assisting, for example, former miners and steelworkers to set up in business. His duties also included working closely with the Prince of Wales's Trust.The extracts chosen from his interview mainly concern Ted's recollection of his family background and formative years in the mining industry. We also have Ted's vivid and sad memories of the 1944 'earth bump' at Barnburgh and the dreadful gas emissions at Barnburgh and Cortonwood (1957 and 1961). The latter, in particular, provides us with an insight in to what it was like to be manager of a colliery when a disaster occurred.

"A good deputy has to have the respect of his men ..."

"My father, also called Ted, one of seven boys, started work in the pit at Featherstone and one of his brothers, Joe, was killed at Goldthorpe on his first day there. Mother came from a family

called Parker who moved to Goldthorpe from Totley and her father worked at Highgate pit where conditions were very wet. He died of pneumonia from working in the damp. Father was an enthusiastic local footballer and could have played professional for First Division Huddersfield but earned more working at Barnburgh. He was a ripper. I had four brothers, two going into mining and two into butchery. For a short period, I had two brothers, four uncles and my father working at Barnburgh (No. 5 pit).

I went to Barnburgh pit a week before I left [Dearnside] school. Father saw me in the yard and asked why I had come, and then sent me away. I went again the Saturday after and saw Mr Hyde, the under-manager. After waiting in a queue, he said, 'What's your name, lad?' I told him Lunness and he asked which one. I said, 'I'm Teddy Lunness's eldest son.' He said, 'Start on Monday.' It was April 1941. I was fourteen.

Edmund Lunness, aged sixteen, with the Dr McLaughlin (First Aid) cup, Worsbrough Bridge, 1943. Ted Lunness

I acquired a hard hat, a snap tin, a bottle and some pit boots on the Saturday – and some old clothes. My mother got me up at 4.45 am, made my breakfast, and I walked it to the pit, meeting people who I knew on the way. My snap was bread and dripping and I took a bottle of tea with no milk. I got my lamp and went down into the pit-bottom where I met a deputy who gave me a job tramming empties from the shaft side, working with two other lads. We did sixty trips per hour and did not stop apart from a twenty-minute snap period. It was cold in the intake shaft bottom. My first wage was 36 shillings and 4 pence for six days' work and I received 6 shillings and 4 pence pocket money.

One evening in September Charlie Chase and myself were walking down Goldthorpe Green, towards Dearnside School and, standing outside was Barnburgh's safety officer, Fred Hall. He was teaching mining subjects there but was a couple of students short for the class to run. He asked us to sign on the course and we agreed. I had started studying. The under-manager got to know that I was going to school and arranged for me to stop working on the haulage and go to the fitting shop, to train to be a fitter.

One day we were having an ambulance practice [Friday 24 April 1942] at the Reform Club, Goldthorpe. Senior members of the brigade were there, along with some members of the rescue team and the medical centre. An urgent message came through – there had been an accident at the pit and ambulance men and rescuers were needed straight away. We juniors tagged along and when we got to the pit I was given a job to take food and water to the base for the rescuers: corned beef sandwiches in a biscuit tin and ten pint dudleys of water. It was an experience. It was classified as a 'big bump', where the strata broke – the *Parkgate* rock – coming down with such a force that caused the floor to come up in the roadways. The floor came up to the roof in places and people were entombed in the workings. There were a lot of very brave men, a lot were rescued [13 men escaped from 17 that were trapped, with 4 men killed]. The men that came out were in a bad state as they had been working in a very hot and dusty area. There were two main entrances to the pit, on Green Lane and Furlong Lane and security people controlled the relatives, sightseers and the press.

The manager allowed me to go to the 'Tech' on Tuesday but only if I did a double shift on the Monday! During that year I did well at school, won a couple of ambulance trophies and a Miners' Welfare Scholarship, so I went to the manager and told him about this and he said that, starting next September, I could go to school and the company would pay my wages. I became one of the first paid part-time day students attending Barnsley Tech.

[At Barnburgh] I was soon sent pony driving. Jet was my favourite horse, named because he was jet-black and a good pony. I collected him from the stables. The pony was fitted with a pair of limmers and took the full tub away, into the pass-by, and when we got ten tubs we dropped them down to the Main Plane where the haulage was, lashed them on to the rope and off they went to the pit-bottom. I was a bit naughty on occasions. I rode the ponies but you got caught. We had two horsekeepers, one of them called George Furness and the other George Green. They would hide in a manhole with whitewash and a brush and splash us as we rode by. We got fined and had to see the under-manager.

I started coalface training and qualified to be a shot-firer. I got all the nasty jobs to begin with, working Saturday nights, doing shot-firing in the main roadways on Sunday afternoons. Bad shifts and bad jobs but I was still only in my early twenties. I was in charge in the *Parkgate seam*. Being in charge of older men did not bother me too much as my family were well known, with a good reputation, so it could have been worse. A good deputy has to have the respect of his men and if he is industrious and he can demonstrate what he is asking other men to do, then everything should be OK. The wages were very good at Barnburgh. It was known as the the pit with the golden pulleys.

They were advertising for overmen at various pits, including Kilnhurst, so I decided to apply, and got the job. I was only twenty-five, living at Thurnscoe with no transport, so I biked it [seven miles)], arriving for 5.30 in the morning. One day I was half an hour late because of heavy snow and got a right telling off. Kilnhurst was a bit on the rough side, the conditions were bad, with inclined seams.

At Kilnhurst I was responsible for the *Parkgate seam* which was hot and not very good. We had a cable belt down there and it was problem with people riding on it. We used to have earth movements or bumps. When the Parkgate rock broke we got heavy pressure causing the floor to lift. I was only there 7–8 months when I got a phone call from one of the senior officials at the Area, Mr Moore, who asked me why I had not applied for the under-manager's job at Barnburgh. I did not know that there was a vacancy as no details had been put on the notice board. I wrote an application and got the job, aged twenty-six. When I started I was put in charge of No 5 pit, the *Barnsley* and *Newhill seams*. I had replaced Tom Hyde, the man who had originally set me on as a fourteen-year-old. The other under-manager was Bob Edwards. He was a real good old pitman who was helpful to me with advice. For a few weeks it was difficult for me. People who knew me from schooldays wanted to be familiar but I had to insist of being addressed in the usual way as 'Mr'. I had my father working for me, [along with] two of my brothers and four uncles.

Soon after I had moved [to Manvers] there was an ignition of gas at Barnburgh, in the part of the pit where I had been previously responsible [26 June 1957, 6 fatalities]. I knew all the men and one of my Uncles, Danny Lunness [aged 48], was killed. It was a very traumatic time as I knew every one of them.

We had an unfortunate emission of gas in the *Silkstone seam* while I was at Cortonwood [June, 1961] and four men suffocated. It happened on a Monday. I went to work for eight in the morning, as usual, and came home about five, had my meal, when the phone rang. It was the under-manager of the *Silkstone*, old Jack Hunter, a wonderful man. He informed me that there had been an emission of gas and all the roadways were full of methane. The rescue teams were sent for but, unfortunately for me, my boss, the group manager, the area deputy production manager and production manager had all gone to a meeting and were not available. I rang Joe Ford, the neighbouring group manager, who had been in charge at Manvers. He, and Fred Steel, the manager at Manvers, came over to assist me. I informed the inspectorate, the police and the press soon got to know. We got the ambulance and rescue men organised as soon as possible. Jack Hunter managed to communicate with some men in the return gate, telling them to turn the compressed air on and to huddle down on the floor. This must have saved their lives but he got no recognition for it. I did not return home until 4 pm the following day;then my boss rang me at home and instructed me to go back to the pit, to be interviewed by the BBC and ITV for the *Six O' Clock News*. I refused as I was exhausted after more than thirty-six hours at work."

(32) Dennis Rodgers

Born: 2 April 1927
Place: Broad Street, Parkgate, Rotherham
Pits: Manvers Main; Wentworth Drift; New Stubbin; Maltby Main
Mining experience: c.1953–1985 (32 years)
Age at interview: 77

I had a lovely relaxed interview with Dennis Rodgers in the back garden of his Maltby home, not far from the big pit where he had spent most of his mining life. I took Dennis to Maltby Main when I went to see him again, only the second time he had been back since his retirement in 1985, not long after the end of the miners' strike. Dennis entered coalmining employment relatively late, at the age of twenty-six, after army service and, having earlier started as an apprentice at the Parkgate Iron and Steel Works. His military career, as a sergeant in the 'Paras', included service in the Middle East. Dennis's baptism to underground work was at Manvers but he soon moved on to work at small and shallow drift mine at the edge of Wentworth village,

Dennis Rodgers, looking relaxed in the back garden of his Maltby home, when interviewed by the author, 22 July 2004. The author

and had a short spell at New Stubbin prior to Maltby where he advanced to become an official.

"... the job was crap [but] *there was always that camararderie with the blokes."*

"I was about twenty-six [1953] when I decided to leave the army but I met an overman, from Manvers Main, in the Travellers pub at Parkgate. I was well qualified due to exams and he advised me to go into mining and 'get my stick and lamp.' The pits needed men then. Because I had mixed with men, the work was quite normal. I did a couple of months training but had a shock when I got to work in the *Parkgate seam*. I got a lump of coal as big as a shed and was told to get it filled before I could go home. Ponies were still being used in the stalls and I was working with a bloke who was seventy-three years old. The face could be 150–200 yards long. It was about five foot ten inches high. I was working in a stint of coal with pick, shovel and hammer – it was all manual. I just wore a pair of shorts.

I only did a year at Manvers before I moved to Wentworth, replacing a man who had got injured. My father-in-law was the union secretary at the pit. It was a good little pit with coal so clean that it did not need washing, a drift, situated on the way to Elsecar. There were only about forty men employed there, including several Polish miners. It was so shallow that water and excreta from the drains [occasionally] seeped through to us. Everything was small scale on the pit-top, just a prefabricated building for the showers. On nights you could even walk out for your snap, cheese and toast on a brazier. Underground, it was all machine work, joy loaders and tractors, with a big jib. We worked in pairs, one driving the loader and one the tractor. One day, with my mate Wilf, I was cutting a junction, near a parked loader at a dead end, and he was breaking in with a seven-foot jib when I heard a mighty crack. I instantly dove out of the way and landed on the side of the conveyor but was buried up to my chin. At first I could not move. Everything went quiet. Then I heard Jimmy Hodge shout to my mate, 'Give over Wilf, he's gone.' My lamp had gone out but I managed to get my hands free and noticed that two wooden props were just holding up a girder. I shouted, 'I'm all right!' Wilf came over this big slurry heap, and I managed to scramble out, leaving my wellies stuck in the mire! The under-manager told me to have a smoke and he would get an ambulance but I insisted that I was OK.

Wentworth Drift closed after I had been there about nine months, so I got a job at New Stubbin. They needed some lads with experience of joy loaders, though I never got to use one there. It was a good little pit with some good lads. It was a cool pit, not too deep. The size of the shaft restricted the amount of coal that could be got out. I was in the *Silkstone seam*, the other one was the *Thorncliffe*. I was ark walling. There was a cutting machine with a jib which normally cut a complete face, I swung it in, and blew the arc out. There was a six-foot, six-inch advance and a wall of coal. The machine was then moved and another six-foot, six-inch was taken out until a new face was made. There were three of us on this job, it was contract work, so we were the best paid men in the pit. Some blokes came to Stubbin from Silverwood and my work stopped. I was put on the market which meant a drop in wages at a time when I had a new mortgage and two kids.

I was always a grafter, so moved on, getting a job at Maltby in July 1964. I was contracting again, packing, and got into a good team. Maltby was a very deep mine. I worked in the *Barnsley seam* with a gang of about thirty men. Bob Finney was the team leader. He was from Parkgate so I knew him. Maltby was doing well but it wasn't easy. The coal was very hard and gassy. It was hot, especially in the waste which could contain a lot of methane. Some men just worked wearing boots – you were always covered in sweat. When refrigerators were introduced some blokes filled big pop bottles with water and stuck them in the fridge, collecting them when they were solid with ice.

I went to see the gaffer and asked him he wanted anyone to train the young lads as I was now forty and experienced. I was set on. It was not easy work, a lot of graft was still needed on the training faces. One day I was working on this rip when just below me was the under-manager, Mr Toft, and a deputy, Les Pittaway. I overheard them talking about the deputies getting a new pay rise. I leaned over and asked Mr Toft if I could see him later and he said it was OK. I asked to be put on the deputys' course. I was forty-three but very fit. I went to [technical] school and passed the exams without any trouble. It was 1972.

My new responsibilities included, first of all, safety. You had to be efficient when reading and interpreting gas percentages, and to be able to deal with the ventilation; I also had to inform people higher up of any problems. First Aid was also very important. I was experienced at handling men from my time in the army but as a deputy you need to act properly. You needed to be cool. Sometimes it was awkward for me when I was placed on someone's shift where there had been bad feelings. I was a deputy for thirteen years.

It was hard going into Maltby pit during the 1984/85 strike. There was always a picket outside the entrance. It became really difficult when pickets came from other pits. I did what I could to help. I picked blackberries and my wife made pies and we would give them to the lads or sell them for a few bob to give [cash] to them. I dished out some of my home coals. I also had some of the lads doing small jobs for me so that I could give them a bob or two. I went

Maltby remains as one of only two surviving deep mines in South Yorkshire (the other being Rossington Main). In the mid 1980s its output was due to increase with the exploitation of the Parkgate *and* Thorncliffe seams, *pending the completion of the sinking of a third shaft.* NCB/Author's collection

Dennis Rodgers back at Maltby Main, August 2004. The author

back to normal work in 1985 but after the year-long strike I had forgotten a lot of the routines. I was suffering from deafness in one ear which made some of the work difficult.

On my last day I walked by the under-manager and he shouted, 'Don't forget to call in, Dennis' but I just put my stuff into the stores and walked up the road. To the gaffers I was just a number. I know that from experience. [But] as much as you can say the job was 'crap', there was always that camaraderie with the blokes. People could get hurt and you always had to help each other."

(33) Len Picken

Born: 19 April 1927
Place: Honeywell Street, Barnsley
Pits: Wharncliffe Woodmoor 4 & 5; Darton Hall ('Pummer'); North Gawber; Wharncliffe Woodmoor 4 & 5; Ferrymoor/Riddings
Mining Experience: 1941–1983 (42 years)
Age at interview: 77

I interviewed Len Picken in his office in Barnsley Town Hall. We struck up a good relationship from the outset and the conversation flowed. Len has been a Labour Councillor for almost twenty years, representing people from the New Lodge area and has a special interest in health and community issues. Len's father, Frank

Councillor Len Picken, Council Chamber, Barnsley Town Hall, 19 November 2004. The author

Picken, worked at 'Sludge' pit [Primrose Colliery], so-called becuase of the wet conditions, and later at Marsden's Paper Mill, working twelve-hour shifts during the war years. Len's Dad had to support a wife, six sons and three daughters, crammed into a two-bedroomed terraced house. After Leaving Raley school at the the the age of fourteen Len obtained a job at Redferns's glassworks, earning 8s. 6d. for a seven-day week. After six months, with a limited amount of money coming into the Picken household, he sought better pay and better prospects in mining. These extracts start with Len describing his early years as a young miner at Wharncliffe Woodmoor 4 & 5 Colliery. After a short spell at a small Darton pit, and a few years at North Gawber, he moved back to 4&5. Now experienced in a variety of practical pit jobs, we hear about his growing capabilities in development work, when creating headings and new drifts, latterly at the modern Ferrymoor/Riddings mine where he became actively involved in union representation.

"I enjoyed working at the pit for the comradeship and knowing that if there was a problem ... someone would ... help me."

"My oldest brother, James Arthur Picken, worked at Wharncliffe Woodmoor 4&5 pit. He asked the under-manager if he could bring me along. I was told what to take, including a bottle of water with some string around the top, so I could tie it to my waistcoat, so it would not fall out. Although the comradeship down the pit was good, men could not afford to give you their water, they could only carry so much. I wore trousers and a shirt, and a soft cap and carried my lamp and anything else that was needed including bread and fat for my snap.

I remember my first day and was frightened to death. I caught a paddy [pit bus] from Honeywell Street and knew most of the men but I was a young lad on my own. My brother took me onto the cage. It was horrible… a double-decker, about twelve on each deck, but sometimes, when men were coming out, there might be sixteen on each! My brother took me from the pit-bottom to the face where he was working as they needed a trammer but the under-manager took one look at me and said that I was far too big for tramming, so I worked in the pit-bottom for about three months, bringing [full] tubs … and coupling on and taking the empties away. There were eight pass-byes to the faces, it was a long way and only tub-high.

Then I went onto a mechanised face, still hand-got coal but cut by a machine. [The face] was bored and fired and you went and filled it off. I was on the next stint to my brother who looked after me. I was sixteen or seventeen. It was very hard work. When I got home I did not have the energy for anything. I was on days and afternoons, but to earn an extra bob or two I worked on a Friday or Saturday night. There were no baths, so I went home in all my pit muck. Mother had to boil everything. I washed my hands and face first and had my meal – and probably fell asleep over it or lay in front of the fire. A bit later she would boil pans of water or used the old set pot and put hot water in the big tin bath.

Eventually I moved away from working with my brother. The unions were very strong at this time. You had to take your turn doing different jobs. I married Margaret [Nicholson] when I was eighteen [in 1948] and we soon started a family, so I had responsibilities. I worked on afters and nights, ripping, coal-cutting, and driving the machines, I could do anything on a regular basis.

I got friendly with Vin Tomlinson and Ted Pearson, two massive men, even compared with my size. They knew the sort of work that I had done and that I was a regular worker, so they asked me to work with them as they were a man short. Nine men worked together on three shifts. I worked on the third shift, back at Wharncliffe Woodmoor 4&5. It was getting highly mechanised by now. They did not want the coal extracting by the shaft, so a drift was driven right from the pit-top into the *Lidget seam* – that's what I worked on with the team. A team called Meakin's started bringing the drift down and we started at the pit-bottom, in the *Beamshaw*, driving up towards them. We met and we were not far out. It was arduous work, standing in water a lot of the time.

In 1970 I was asked to go to Riddings Drift and all my men went with me. Access was in South Kirkby pit yard. The coal came from Ferrymoor pit [Grimethorpe] so there were a lot of union discussions to sort things out. It was eventually named Ferrymoor/Riddings. We had no union representation [there] and I wasn't such a political animal as I am now but I knew where I stood when the pit's name changed, so special dispensation was given for someone from Riddings to be on the union. They were all Ferrymoor men at the time and I was elected. Then I became a committee man and the treasurer. It was a very cosmopolitan pit, men from all over working there. The Secretary and myself split our responsibilities and I looked after the Barnsley area men.

I never wanted to be a deputy, could never go around bossing men but I got on well with them; but I did not mind being in charge of my own team. In development work we were experts in strata and I could be boring, sometimes in rock or it could be coal or shale. As a chargehand, I could handle powder and detonators. Some of the managers were OK, others

Len Picken (centre) with Chairman of the National Coal Board, Alfred Robens (Lord Robens of Woldingham) in the new Riddings Drift (South Kirkby linked to Ferrymoor, Grimethorpe) c.1969. In 1973 Riddings Drift merged with Ferrymoor to create what was called the Ferrymoor/Riddings unit. Len Picken/NCB

not so good. When I first started I can not remember calling anyone 'Mr' apart from the under-manager and manager. The managers knew my first name, they were good at remembering so many names. I think that I was respected down the pit, doing all that development and drift work, they were always big projects.

I enjoyed working at the pit for the comradeship and also knowing that if I had got a problem I had always got someone there to help me. Most of the time when I was on the union lads would come to me with their problems, things that were personal to them. I enjoyed doing this work and, after I had retired, decided to stand as a Councillor because I wanted to continue my interest in the welfare of people."

Len Picken (third right) and NCB Chairman Derek Ezra (second right) looking at plans for the new East Side Coal Preparation Plant serving Ferrymoor/Riddings and South Kirkby collieries, c.1973. Len Picken/NCB

(34) Arthur Wakefield

Born: 5 May 1928
Place: South Hiendley, West Yorkshire
Pits: South Kirkby; Monckton (No 3); South Kirkby; Ferrymoor(Grimethorpe); South Elmsall
Mining experience: 1941–1985 (44 years)
Age at interview: 73

My first meeting with Arthur Wakefield took place in 2001 when we talked about the diary and scapbooks that he compiled during the 1984/85 miners' strike. The subsequent publication (now in its second reprint) of *Miners' Strike Day by Day* was a great

Former South Elmsall miner Arthur Wakefield in the garden of his South Kirkby home, with his Yorkshire terrier, Tina, summer 2004. The author

success, an important contribution to the last great industrial dispute of modern times. Small in stature but big in heart, and a tenor voice, Arthur is a much respected figure in and around the former mining communities of South Elmsall. The son of a miner, Arthur recalled his father picking coal from South Kirkby muckstack during the 1930s when many pitmen were reduced to short-time work. The interview extracts included here begin with Arthur's memories of leaving school, in 1942, aged fourteen, continue with a description of his early pit-work and conclude with a personal insight into the dramatic end of the 1984/85 strike.

"It was a fight against pit closures, and therefore in the long term was for my grandchildren ..."

"Prior to leaving school [c.1942], the teacher asked all the boys how many of us were going down the coal-mine and at least seventy-five per cent put their hand up. I wanted to be a jockey as I was only five foot high and weighed five stones. I could hardly look over the tubs. We had three weeks training at Acton Hall colliery which, with South Kirkby and Hemsworth was part of the same company. My first week's wages were £3. 2s. 6d. and I got the 2s. 6d. as pocket money!

I remember my first ride down the shaft, it was frightening – my belly was in my mouth, what a sensation. First of all, I stayed in the pit-bottom and coupled empty tubs together. Then I did a job called 'clamming-on'. After so many tubs were coupled together they would be clammed [fastened] and taken somewhere else, into a pass-by. They would then be taken to the coalface. After so long in that pit-bottom area I was told to go down the road[way]s, further towards the coalfaces. I did a bit of clamming-on down there but the main job was with the binders, which meant you had to be observant. The binders were on part of a roadway round a bend and the endless haulage rope was around five pulleys so you had to see that the rope stopped on the pulleys. I used a 'stang' [iron bar] and put it at the back end of the run, near the clam or clip, kept it down so that the weight of the tubs at the back-end did not pull the rope off the pulleys. That was for the empties. Now the full ones, when they come up, I had two lamps, one for my use and one to hang up. When I did not see that light it meant there was a run of full tubs coming so I had to go down and take the end clip or clam off the tubs because if it would not go round the pulley, it would pull the rope off. I was on my own all day.

In 1948 I transferred to South Elmsall, a pit on its own but in the same yard as Frickley. I had heard many reports that it was a good little pit. It was also known as No 3 pit and Shafton pit as it worked the *Shafton seam*, [which was] about four-foot six inches and very wet. That was the first pit where I saw conveyor belts. I did three weeks on the pit-top first as there was no vacancy underground, but every snap time I knocked on the manager's [Mr Hedley's] door. I worked for two years on the haulage, before starting coalface training – we did about a hundred days, stinting with a man who was supervising, also on waste work, packing. A team of two men had two packs and two bays, putting the packs on and drawing the supports out. After training we went on what was called the 'Note' where we got the same money as the man you were working with. As I said, there was water in the workings, a lot underfoot. At first, when I was training, it was a little bit frightening because you got the weight coming on, the sound of thunder, so you wondered what was happening but we were told that everything was all right and not to worry as it would stop after a while. It was the sound of the waste or gob breaking when the supports were taken out. You could hear props cracking, it was frightening.

I kept a diary during the 1984/85 strike. I just missed out of being finished at South Elmsall colliery but I thought to myself I haven't really finished, I am still employed. It was a fight about pit closures and therefore in the long term it was for my grandchildren, so I thought that I was as much involved as anyone. I backed my Union and I thought it was my duty to support them. When volunteers were asked for picket duty I put my name down. Some miners might have said that they did their stint in 1974 and that was it but it was my view was that as long as you were employed and in the Union you should support it. I don't think that I missed a day picketing or collecting. I never got involved in harming any working miner. There was just that laughable incident when I was going to paint SCAB on the front gate of the scab, in the same street where I had lived for twenty-five years. The scab's wife used to come round with the football coupon. Occasionally, I took mine to her if we had been out shopping. I asked her what she thought about Arthur Scargill and she told me that her husband did not think much to him. I told her I thought he was doing a great job for the miners, a fighter. This was just before the strike. When I heard that there was a scab in that street I knew who it was. Margaret, my wife, would not have agreed for me to do anything against other miners but I decided to go ahead. I got a tin of paint and crouched down below their privet hedge until I reached their front gate and started writing SCAB in white paint on the causeway by the gate. I just got the 'S' done when there was a shout: 'WHAT ARE YOU DOING? There were two of them, one with a baseball bat. They had been waiting for me. They chased me but I decided to stand my

ground and turned around. I told them that if they made an attempt to hit me with that baseball bat then I will throw the can of paint in their faces. I asked the scab why he had returned to work and he said that he could not live on hand-outs. I told him that breaking a strike was a very serious matter and that there was no excuse. Someone opened a bedroom window and shouted to see if I was all right. I said I was OK and we dispersed. I got some paint on my winter coat. I thought that I had better tell Margaret what had happened as I would expect a visit since one of the persons who chased me was married to the scab's daughter and was the community policeman. About ten the next morning there was a knock on my door. I was told that I should not have done it and I was summonsed to go to the court at Pontefract. As I entered a room by the court I met a local JP who

Arthur Wakefield signing copies of the book The Miners' Strike Day by Day, *based on the diary that he kept during the 1984/85 dispute, Selby, March 2002.* The author

was a miner. A big policeman put his hand on my shoulders and said, 'Don't you think you want to forget about this scab situation and put it behind you?' I told him no, never in a million years. I got bound over for twelve months.

I felt really sick when the strike ended. I was a member of the Houghton Main Male Voice Choir for sixteen years. We used to go to Sheffield City Hall to do a concert with other choirs. We met on that particular night and there was a brass band presentation at the same time. It was brilliant. Our conductor, from London, stopped the performance, and it went very quiet. I was first tenor, at the front. It was announced that the strike had been called off. It was over but there was no agreement. It was just as though a great iron demolition ball had hit me in the stomach. I felt sick as a dog. Twelve months. We did not expect getting everything that we wanted but there was no compromise. The NCB would not even negotiate because there were so many working miners going in.

We all went back after the strike but not on the first day because some Kent miners had come up to the Frickley picket, having walked it from Bettshanger on the day of the march back to work. There were banners and bands. I said that if there were Kent pickets at the pit yard then I would not cross the line. I went at the front of the procession, on my own, walking down the High Street. The Kent men had a picket line so I turned around as the main body arrived and put my hands in the air and shouted 'YOU DO NOT CROSS THE PICKET LINE!' We did not go back to work that day but there was a meeting with the Kent men who then agreed not to picket."

(35) James Reeve

Born: 5 October 1928
Place: Firbeck Street, Denaby Main
Pits: Cadeby; Denaby Main; Cadeby; Barnburgh [Assistant Manager/Personnel]; Maltby [Assistant Manager/Planning & under-manager]; Thurcroft [Under-manager]; South Yorks Area HQ [Strata Control Engineer]
Mining experience: 1942–1985 (43 years)
Age at interview: 75

Jim Reeve was extremely well prepared when I went to see him at his Conisbrough home, in July 2004. He had carefully produced a detailed summary of his mining experiences and appointments, covering more than forty years. The following extracts concentrate on Jim's early experiences as a young surveyor at Cadeby

Jim Reeve photographed by the author in the garden of his Conisbrough home, 19 May 2004.
The author

and Denaby Main. By 1958 he was back at Cadeby, soon to be working as a deputy and overman. Always interested and active in matters relating to first aid and safety, I have also referred to Jim's work in the Mines Rescue Service, in particular that awful day in 1961 when four men were killed at Cortonwood. Some aspects of Jim's later managerial career are also included. After his retirement, Jim has been very active in a number of community matters relating to the Denaby-Conisbrough areas.

"I got very interested in surveying …"

"I was fourteen when I left [Conisbrough Modern] school. I went home on the Friday night and on the Saturday morning dad took me across to Cadeby pit. We lived in Balby Street then, just across from the colliery. I thought that I might become an electrician but there were no vacancies. On our way back we bumped into Len Harvey, one of the senior overmen, an excellent mining engineer, and he told Dad that he was looking for a boy to join the survey staff. Mum took me to Whitaker's on the main road and bought me a pair of pit boots. I had then to find some old clothes.

I started on the Monday. I did not have a cap but I was advised to wear a protective helmet though it was not compulsory in those days. My Dad sorted me a locker and we got changed. We had to walk to the shaft on the surface all the way from the lamp room, past the pump room and up four or five decks of steps leading to the shaft side. When we got there Ernest Hanwell, a deputy and qualified surveyor, looked after me. The cage was four decks but there were only Ernest, Dad and myself in one of them. I was told to hold tight, it lifted up and down we went. I will never forget it. The speed fascinated me but I wondered if it would stop! I was nervous and when we got half way down I felt sure that we were coming back up, a sensation that was quite common.

On my first day Dad took me to the box hole and left me with the pit-bottom deputy. After all the men had gone forward he gave me a sweeping brush! I had to sweep the box hole out and then the nearby roadways. It was done to get me used to the pit-bottom and to get my underground eyesight. The first day seemed an eternity.

One of my first jobs was to go to the stables and mix a small can of whitewash. We painted white lines on the roof so as to keep the route of roadways straight. I had a little paint pot and tripod to carry. The surveyors were good chaps. Horace Corbett was the main surveyor. From time to time we had people coming from the survey department of the Amalgamated Denaby Colliery Company and got to know them (for example Roy Carling and Hugh Lindsey). I learnt a lot in the first few years and started evening classes, at Conisbrough Modern School.

I worked in all parts of the colliery. The main seams were the *Barnsley* and the *Parkgate*. The *Barnsley* consisted of the Middle East, East Low Side, North East 1 and the South District; then there was a section called the Barnsley Landing. The *Parkgate* was a lot different. The ventilation in the *Barnsley* was reasonable but the deeper *Parkgate*, reached by an underground drift, was very warm and humid. I remember when I was about sixteen and Horace informed me that we were going down the South District [where the 1912 Cadeby disaster occurred]. It was hot there. We came to an old roadway and went through a ventilation door and you could see old tub rails, a flatsheet and the rails were hot to touch. We spent an hour and a half there, completing measurements. Coming out this area, you could feel a much better atmosphere.

I got very interested in surveying and at Denaby Main they wanted a young man to be the assistant surveyor, so I transferred, in April 1947, a few months after nationalisation. Denaby also worked the *Parkgate* and *Barnsley seams*. To get to the *Barnsley* workings you had a long hike down the Montagu Plane and when you got to the main districts it was a longwall face, about three-quarters of a mile long, divided into stalls. Coal was hand-filled into tubs. The men started at one end of the stall and worked the coal back – they knew how to work it by the lay of the seam. It was six foot, a good height, and the seam had some 'tops' and a two to four-inch dirt band but it was a good seam. They used picks, crow bars and shovels, working stripped to the waist. My job was to put lines on the face, to keep the stalls straight; also to keep the roadways straight, also putting a line on the gate-ends. It involved a lot of walking but we decided to go to work earlier than eight, which meant that we could catch the paddy mail and get a ride.

The *Parkgate* was a more modern seam, especially on the North side of the pit where there were conveyers, Panzas and machines that fitted on top of them, and disks came in. It was about four-foot on average, with a good solid rock top. Chocks were introduced. It was all fully mechanised and they even tried American-style working, using shuttle cars, which was very interesting. On the South side of the *Parkgate* there were conveyers and still filled by hand. On the North East they did partial extraction with shaker pans and a cutter. On the West side coal was extracted between three roads and it was hand-filled, so there was a big variation in working.

As a surveyor I had to help measure up when an accident had occurred, to prepare plans, especially if there was an inquest and for the mines inspector. George Teasdale was the chief surveyor at Denaby, a smashing chap. One Sunday a deputy got killed. The Dr arrived and I took him on a long walk to the *Barnsley seam,* carrying his bag. We met the stretcher party and the man was pronounced dead. These were very sad occasions. On another occasion a piece of rock had fallen and trapped a man's head at the side of a conveyer. It was very upsetting to see, but part of the job.

I had not succeeded passing my written exams and I had a difference of opinion with the manager. Supported by the NUM, I decided to do my coalface training and moved back to Cadeby in October 1958. I managed OK and was offered a shot-firer's job. For this experience I worked with Mick Hudson, an old-style deputy who was very helpful. My surveying experience was an advantage as I was able to mark the gate lines for him and on Friday nights I used to help him with the wages.

In 1960 I was a deputy, following experience working in the *Dunsil seam,* working nights for eighteen months. One of the main attributes of a good deputy is to be honest with the men. You should not try to kid them. If they have done the work then they should get paid accordingly but if they haven't then they should not. I never had any trouble by being honest.

I became interested in the Mines Rescue Service before returning to Cadeby. You had to be fit and able. I went through a course, passed and practised at Rotherham's Mines Rescue Station, St Annes Road. I started with the Denaby team and then joined the Cadeby team. On one occasion [in 1961], when I was on nights, the colliery manager and his man arrived at our house to call me out. My wife, who was heavily pregnant, got up and told them I was in the pit. I received a message to come out of the pit and thought it was a problem with my wife's pregnancy. I got into the van, everybody waiting, and off we went to Cortonwood. When we arrived the local team and other teams were already there. We waited and were eventually required to go underground in the morning. The first thing we saw was one of the bodies

Cadeby Colliery Officials football team, 1960. Back row (L-R): A Dodd, A Hawking, J Reeve, C Senior, P Bradwell and W Globe; front row: C Green, R Sapey, A Tuke, R Callandine and R Cory. Jim Reeve

being brought out on a stretcher, which was very upsetting [4 miners were killed when gas escaped into workings]. We continued to the next station, then to another but it was virtually all over. We removed some tackle and it was about 2 pm by the time we got back to Cadeby. My wife did not know where I had been! Afterwards, a new system was introduced, a board at the pit showed if the rescue team member was at work or at home.

In 1967 adverts appeared for personnel managers and I decided to apply, [and was] interviewed at Coal House in Doncaster. I was successful and started a short training course to get to know all the departments and offices. I started in April and, by December, was posted to Barnburgh Colliery where I stayed for three years. Absenteeism was the biggest problem, so we set up a committee which consisted of the NUM, NACODS and myself and had some success. The managers had a 'sack 'em' attitude but too many good men would have been lost if that had operated. Many absentee problems were solved by consultation.

I remember one morning when I got to the pit there had been a fatality, involving a deputy who had got tangled with a disk drum. We satisfied ourselves who the man was and it was up to myself and the nurse to go and tell his family. This was my worst experience in mining. To tell a man's wife and daughter that he would not be coming home was very distressing.

I moved to Maltby in January 1971, appointed as assistant manager, and in November 1972 was appointed colliery under-manager. Maltby pit was a lot different to what I had been used to. It was deep and fully mechanised and a tough pit to manage. I was there during the 1972 and 1974 strikes but knew some of the pickets who came there from Cadeby and everything was OK. On the whole I got on well with the men. Some of the face conditions were excellent. When everything went well on a rich face it was great but when things went wrong it could be a nightmare to sort out.

My next move was to Thurcroft, in October 1977, as colliery under-manager. Thurcroft was a family pit where everybody co-operated and there were few problems."

IV
Born After 1931

'GOING HOME'

(36) Arthur Nixon

Born: 30 April 1931
Place: Barnsley
Pits: North Gawber; Houghton Main; Wombwell Main; Woolley; North Gawber; Grimethorpe; Wharncliffe Woodmoor 4 & 5
Mining experience: c.1945–1960 (c.15 years)
Age at interview: 73

Arthur Nixon has lived and worked in Essex and Norfolk for many years but his early working life was spent in several Barnsley area pits. He contacted me in 2002 with a query concerning Houghton Main and was in the process of compiling an audio tape, for his children, about his mining experiences.

Arthur Nixon who, following his mining experiences at several Barnsley pits, joined the RAF and then moved on to a career in occupational therapy prior to setting up his own business. Arthur Nixon

The extracts are taken from this recording in which Arthur describes his experiences as a young electrician and his work on coal-cutting machines. Following service in the RAF, Arthur worked in engineering, and in an occupational therapy department. In 1995, he started his own business, after patenting a chair-lifting gadget, his son, Philip, is now in charge.

"My first job was to lubricate coal-cutting machines and conveyor belt gears."

"I left [Raley] school when I was fourteen, in 1945, and had a short spell of employment with a Worsbrough Dale plumber, earning eighteen bob a week, but the prospects of earning a good living were not promising. My friends worked in the pits and were making good money so I decided to go into the mining industry. I was interested in science and decided to apply to be an electrician, so I went on my bike to Staincross one foggy day, to North Gawber pit yard and was directed to the manager's office, reached by some steps, alongside some other offices. I knocked on the door and and a voice called out 'Come in'. There were about six chaps inside,

Arthur Nixon, not long before he left Raley School, Barnsley, aged fourteen, in 1945. Arthur Nixon

in their pit muck, sat around a table, with a roaring fire. The manager said, 'Now then lad, what can I do for you?' I told him that I was looking for a job. 'What sort of job?' he said. I asked if if there was a job for me in the electric shop. He looked at me and replied, 'Are tha religious?' I said, 'We'll I went to Sunday school but that's all.' He said that there were a lot of Bible-punchers down there but he gave me a note and sent me to speak to Fred Moxon, the pit engineer. He asked me a few questions and asked me when I could start. I think I started immediately, the next day.

I was sent to Woolley Colliery where there was an underground training gallery. We learnt to locker-up tubs, deal with a pony, test for gas, lash-on tubs with a chain and a clam. I also attended Barnsley Mining & Technical College. I was keen to go underground, mainly because you got better money and I would be working with electricians, learning a trade. At the time a lot of men were returning from war service. My first job was to lubricate coal-cutting machines and conveyor belt gears. I had to fill two gallon cans with thick gear oil. I had to get to the face before the colliers arrived. Once the shaker pans had started, metal troughs running the length of the face, shook back and forward and shook the coal down as it was shovelled on by the colliers. I scrambled into the 'stable' where the machine had been left and had to clean debris from the top of it and then it was a difficult job to get the oil into the machine as there was not much roof space. I was fortunate at having a cap lamp, on a peaked canvas cap, fed from a battery on my belt. Once I was riding on the shakers when my light went out so I dove off and had to make my way out of the pit, using an oil lamp, but I had lost my oil cans, so had to go out of the pit and get some new ones. This was under privatisation when the pit was owned by Sir William Sutherland. The *Top Haigh Moor seam* was about two foot six inches thick and had solid rock above but the *Low Haigh Moor seam* was soft shale where a previous manager, Mr Weaver, was killed by a roof fall. The manager when I was there was called Mr Scott who lost his life on a conveyor belt accident.

In 1947 I moved to Houghton Main where modern machinery were being used and got a job in the electric shop. I was taken to see the No 1 shaft steam winder, an impressive thing, immaculately clean. I was with electrician John Graham and was to work in the *Barnsley seam* which was seven foot of solid coal. They were removing shaft pillars, taking out coal as safely as possible and machines had been brought from America, enormous shuttle cars. The joy loader had arms and shovelled into the coal, loading four tons a minute. It was on tracks like a tank. the jib could be raised and lowered and swung from side to side and had red reflectors, so looked like a dragon with red eyes in the light of your cap lamp. The special boring machine drilled holes that used cardox shells instead of powder, about a yard long and two inches diameter and released a charge of gas that broke up the coal. It was loaded with the joy loader which moved on tracks like a tank. The coal was then loaded into the shuttle cars which had conveyors at the bottom. The cars were run on large 24-cell batteries, weighing a ton each, charged with a generator in the pit-bottom. It was a quite exciting situation but, once the loader got going, the dust was incredible and you could hardly see. Coal was taken on to a loader and on to a conveyor belt and into tubs to the pit-bottom and out.

I moved on to Wombwell Main, working on a water infusion project which involved boring holes into the coalface. The coal was hand-got, they used pneumatic picks and shovels, shifting the coal that way but there was a heck of a lot of dust so a suppression method involving boring series of holes and pumped in high pressure water which dampened the coal, though the colliers did not like it as it made the coal difficult to shift. As time moved on I thought about getting a job out of the pit but, in 1952, got my call up for National Service. I decided to sign for an extra year which gave me a trade and married quarters. Before going into the army I worked for short while at Woolley pit, on a Sampson coal-cutting machine which was on skids which raised it about eighteen inches in order to cut out a dirt band between two layers of coal.

I served in the Royal Signals until March 1955. I had a short spell out of the pit after the army, but the wage was poor, so I went back to North Gawber colliery where I operated a coal-cutting machine.

I then managed to get a job at Grimethorpe as they were using the same type of machines that I had worked on at Houghton Main. At first the miners did not believe the 4-tons a minute rate of the machines. Finally, I finished up at Carlton, at Wharncliffe Woodmoor 4 & 5 pit, working as a coal-cutter operator in the *Kent seam*. I worked with a younger lad on an Ace cutter. We tried to obtain tungsten carbide tipped picks so they would last longer and we had a 'peggy' tool made up, hammer-head at one end and a sharpened pick at the other. By then power-loaders were being introduced but there was a lot of resistance to using them. There was talk about coal stock piles and pit closures."

(37) Terry Carter

Born: 11 June 1931
Place: Harrow Street, Moorthorpe, South Elmsall
Pit: Frickley Colliery
Work: 1946–1985 (39 years)
Age at interview: 72

Terry is one of fourteen children from the marriage of Thomas and Martha Carter. Thomas was born in Ireland during the 1880s and served in South Africa during the Boer War. Moving to Yorkshire from Lancashire, he was one of the first miners to work at Frickley Colliery [sunk 1903–5], but volunteered for further army service during the Great War [achieving the rank of sergeant major], survived a 'gassing' in France and returned to pitwork. Terry thus recalls a very disciplined childhood. Terry did not immediately follow his father's footsteps, finding work on the Warde Aldham estate at Hooton Pagnell but after a year he was heading for Dad's pit. From working on the pit-

Terry Carter, who spent almost all of his working life at Frickley Colliery. The author

top screens to 'road laying' underground, Terry describes some of the most memorable aspects of his mining life, including an unofficial and unforgettable ascent of No. 2 shaft.

"Once I experienced a shock when coming up the cage.."

"I went to Frickley pit in 1946 and I had no problems in signing on straight away. I remember my first day. It was six o'clock day shift, so I was up about 4.30 to 5 am. My mam had already cut my snap which, mostly, was dripping with plenty of salt on. I also took a glass bottle of tea. There was a snap cabin with a roaring fire and we put our bottle there to keep the tea warm. As soon as that buzzer started the work started and I was picking muck off the belts [on the screens]. You had never seen dust like it! The men there were old or had suffered injuries down the pit. There was a man in

Terry Carter, from a school photograph taken in 1940. Terry Carter

charge but we used to throw lumps of coal at him but he found out and threw some back! I worked on the screens for a while but anytime I could get to work on the pit hill I took the opportunity. First of all I shoved empties round and eventually I did every job there was there, doing a man's job at sixteen, on the tipler. When pits were nationalised in 1947, on Vesting Day, I was on the screens, on afternoons, and every wagon in the yard – some were made at the pit in its own wagon shop but many of them came from all over England, with different names and numbers on them, so when I filled a wagon we had to write the numbers down and pass this information to the checkweigh but on that day I was with a washer. On this day the foreman came round and told us not to bother as normal but just open the hoppers. They used to stop winding at 9.30 pm and you did not put your check in until 10 o'clock and that night there wasn't a wagon in the yard but after midnight everything that was in the pit yard belonged to the NCB. The pit-top went on nights for the first time, with only two coaling shifts, days and afters, but when they put the skip in they were winding coal twenty-four hours a day.

I would not go underground as I wanted to be a footballer as it was a big interest and I was a decent player. I did not want to gobble any more dust into my lungs. I wanted to be fit. In the early 1950s everybody was being called up, even those on the pit-top, but you were exempt if you worked down the pit. I was in my early twenties when I went to work underground but I had been down before. We had to go for six weeks to Grimethorpe Colliery, and that is where I first went underground.

My first job was at No.1 pit-bottom and it was colder than the North Pole! On the bottom deck where I worked it was about five foot high. My job, when coal was on the chair – there were two decks – six Barnsley tubs on a deck, we used to have to knock six empties off, couple them on and send them down the different roads. Afterwards I had various jobs in the pit-bottom. There was a long waiting list to get out of the pit-bottom as it was warmer in other parts and better money. Eventually, I went on the haulage which was at the other side of the pit, on the west side. Tubs used to come from the pit-bottom with all the supplies in such as timber and trams of rings and, lashing them on to a rope, I took them down to the face and they would be knocked off and I would take the empties back. After a period of time me and my mate had to work as road-layers, laying the iron rails down for the tubs even though we knew little about the job. The rails had to be extended to the faces. We got about a pound a day more money on this job. I finished up road laying.

Once I experienced a shock when coming up the cage … they had electrified No 2 and I was in the roadlayers and had to come out and I used to occasionally come up and have a cup of tea and a smoke and go back down but on this day they had put electric winding on and every day this firm from Doncaster would arrive and used to take the shaft for about two hours and they had not quite got the hang of it because there were a few incidents. Anyway, I asked if I was OK for the draw that was going up, before they took it otherwise it was a waste of time. Gates were put at each side when men were riding. There was only me on, I was in the middle of the chair and got hold of the rail, gradually the speed increased but it was going faster than normal and it stopped dead … my mind went blank..and my stomach was upset … I just held on and it was terrifying … what I learnt afterwards was that I was not supposed to be on the chair and the winder didn't know I was there. When it stopped … it seemed like ten minutes to me … I was panicking. I though that if it starts dropping down I'll have to take a running jump and try and grab on to a cable at the side of the shaft … anyway it started going up, slowly, and when I got to the pit-top banksman came and asked me what I was doing on the

Terry was a promising young footballer, his favourite position for Moorthorpe Juniors was inside-right or on the right wing. Terry Carter

chair! I went home as I was so shook up. I daren't go to the ambulance room as I should not have been on the chair. It gave me a real scare.

I was out on strike a year in 1984/85. It was very rough. When the scabs started to go back, late on, I went picketing at my own pit, going every morning. On the first morning that we went there was a right battle ... there were six or eight police vans on Westfield Lane ... I turned round and saw police horses charging so I had to get away by a side road ...

I worked about six months after the strike. I was walking down the gantry one day and an under-manager said to me 'Look, we have the power now.' I told him that he had no brains to use any power. He asked for my name but I only gave my check

Moorthorpe Juniors, c.1948. Terry Carter is seated, on the front row of the players, first left. Terry Carter

number so that he would have to find it out. It was difficult to argue with them as they had the upper hand.

In my life as a miner I met some great blokes and I had some great comradeship ... we had to look after each other because of safety. It would have been terrible but for that friendship with my mates as the conditions of work could be obscene. I have seen men working naked except for wearing a belt, it was so hot down some of the districts such as the Hooton Seam which was very productive but gassy.

I wore my ordinary old clothes but some warm ones at the pit-bottom. I wore clogs for a long time. After the NCB took over safety boots became compulsory and they could be bought at reduced price from the stores but eventually became free. Helmets were not compulsory to begin with. Men used to wear flat caps. There were no masks for many years. When I first started there were about 3,000 men employed at the pit so lockers had to be provided for them in the baths. I shared with my uncle and my nephew and when we were on the same shift, on days, most of the pit were on days, it was very crowded!"

(38) Robert 'Bob' Jackson

Born: 1 August 1931
Place: No Place, Beamish, County Durham
Pits: Margaret(Tanfield Lea, Durham); New Stubbin (Rawmarsh); Margaret(Tanfield Lea); New Stubbin
Mining experience: 1945–1949; 1951–1976 (c.29 years)
Age at interview: 73

Many Geordies found work in Yorkshire pits. For some the transition went well but for others it was far from smooth. In this interview, Bob Jackson talked about his family background at No Place in County Durham, and his first job, working on the screens and, later, pony driving at the Margaret pit. Bob admitted to me that it was difficult for him to be 'accepted' when he moved to New Stubbin. The only way he could get face training was by returning to his home pit. Back at Stubbin, and now qualified, he did a variety of jobs but never felt comfortable. Nevertheless, he describes his experiences with a good deal of humour.

Robert Jackson who came from a Durham mining family, moving to Rawmarsh and employment at New Stubbin Colliery, photographed on 27 July 2004. The author

"I got my leg pulled a bit because I was a Geordie."

"My father [John George Jackson] worked at several pits from the age of thirteen but the one that I can remember is Burns' pit where there was a big explosion and a lot of people killed, and many men out of work for about five years. Father then received just ten shillings a week with five children at home to feed, but there were nine children altogether. He was a tall thin man who loved his work and a pint of beer but died aged fifty-four, suffering from lung disease.

The houses in No Place were private, arranged in streets but when we moved to Tanfield Lea pit, we lived in pit houses. Down the street was my Aunt Emma Jane, just four doors away. We got what was left on a Monday from their Sunday dinner. Then there was my Uncle Charlie who lived further down, they were all out of work at the same time. There were five rows of houses with about fifty in each street, and a billiard hall. There was nowhere to go. Burns was in Stanley, two miles away and Tanfield Lea pit was five miles away. He had to walk. He was a ripper. It was only sixteen inches high where he worked. When my brother, Bill, was sixteen he was finishing his shift when at Timperley when there was a flood, two seams flooded. They took all the horses out before they let the men out who who wearing just shorts and vests.

I left school when I was fourteen and my first job was at Euwood's, getting sixteen shillings a week but my bus fare was five shillings. After my mother got her bit there was nothing left for me. I was going into engineering. My brother had got a job as a welder there and I had to go to school as well. After twelve months it was the thin edge of the wedge. Euwoods were getting work for nothing, young lads employed on the rollers, on poor pay. I had had enough.

I got set on at Tanfield Lea (Margaret's) pit. My first job was working on the screens. You needed a shovel by your side ready for when someone shouted 'Stones coming!' I worked with some old miners and young lads that were under-aged. The boss was about sixty-four and a right miserable bloke. I was on the screens about a year, until I was sixteen, old enough to go down the pit.

My first job was in the pit-bottom, pony driving. My father told me to see the stableman and get a different horse as mine was very difficult. It was called Bolt! I had had to run twice, nearly back to the stables to catch him. He went up into another seam. My next horse was a lovely one called Dream but someone had spoilt him when he was broken in. The shafts were not placed on properly so it caught the horse's haunches when it was unattached to a tub so it would run away fast, back to the other end of the landing where it would get an empty put on. The only way that I used to manage was to take his reigns and put one onto one of the handles and that used to stop him. It took me some time to get him right. A bloke called Mordue was overman. I was fed up one day as my lamp kept going out and it was a job to get it lit, so I told him that I was going home. He told me that he would tell my father but I said that I did not care. It was terrible when your lamp went out and I had to feel my way down to the place where you could get it lit. He gave me his electric light and I was given one the next day. I was pony driving until I was eighteen.

I came to live in Rawmarsh, where my wife came from, and found a job at New Stubbin pit. I had been to see the recruiting man who told me that there was always a job for young lads. I was used to main and tail haulage but here it was where they put it on the front and fastened it onto a rope with a clamp and chain, four tubs at a time. The clamp was fastened to a rope. [The] main and tail [gate] has a landing – you put thirty tubs in the landing, one side for empties, one for full ones … you ran thirty empties into the landing, put the ropes onto the full ones and sent them back to the pit-bottom. I then went into the workings, onto the loader ends, shoving the tubs underneath. It was terrible with dust and the money was still poor so I did not like it. You could not have a minute, just working all the time.

My next job was taking supplies such as girders down to the faces. There was an old bloke called 'Stumpy' Price who liked doing overtime and used to say to me 'We'll get some overtime out of this job, Bob'. But, to me, I only wanted to finish and get out of the pit as soon as I could. Things changed though after my son, Robert, was born. For the following ten days me and Stumpy did loads of overtime! I needed the money.

I was on strike once at Stubbin, for a day, when fish got in the tap water! There were about ten taps and the end of the baths where we would fill our dudleys but on this particular day there were little fish in the water. They had got in through the filters. The baths were good but I did not like to see men smoking on the pit-top, especially in the showers.

I got my leg pulled a bit because I was a Geordie. I did not like that too much and at times I could be hot-tempered. I needed a better paid job now that I had family responsibilities so asked about face training. I was told I would not get it as I was a 'foreigner', in other words that I did not come from around Rawmarsh and that it was the local lads who would get the training. I decided to go back home which I did for eighteen months, leaving my wife at Rawmarsh for some of the time. I got my training done at Tanfield Lea and then returned to Rawmarsh. At the time the 'Canyon' pit houses were being built and more houses were built at Elsecar for newcomers from places such as Scotland, Wales and the North East. I got set on again at Stubbin, working on the face, after showing them my qualifications. I was hanging belts, and then machines came in. The faces could be two hundred yards, a hundred yards on each side. I was on the same shift as the cutter but became a utility man: in other words, can you do this, can you do that, all the awkward jobs. Once I got to know how to do a job I was put on another one. I was regarded as an outsider. If anyone was off they would send for me to do the drilling on the face or any dinting that had to be done. I had to pull all the machine cables up everyday, had dints to do and girders to place and make sure the wheels were OK. I was forty-five when I decided to finish and had had enough."

(39) Eric Crabtree

Born: 13 July 1932
Place: Highfield Road, Conisbrough
Pit: Cadeby
Mining experience: c.1947–1985 (38 years)
Age at interview: 72

Eric Crabtree's father, George, worked at Cadeby all his working life, apart from a short spell in the 1920s at Maltby Colliery, eventually contracting, as a ripper. His maternal grandfather, Turton Hagas, was killed in an underground accident at Featherstone Main, aged forty. Prior to this he had been actively involved in organising union activities but was sacked and blacklisted for his efforts by the coal

Former Cadeby miner Eric Crabtree at his Conisbrough home, 12 May 2004. The author

owners. Turton's son also died aged forty in an accident at the Prince of Wales Colliery, Pontefract. Eric's first job, in the exceptional winter of 1947, was as a fitter at the Consibrough brickworks but, after a few months and, 'against Dad's advice', he decided to move to the pit. After six months training Eric was working at the 'motorhouse', a great engine situated about a quarter of mile from the pit-bottom, reacting to signals. In this extract Eric describes his subsequent work as a young 'air and dust tester' when he soon got to know the underground layout of the colliery, including the old workings where eight-eight men and boys lost their lives in the terrible disaster of 1912. He also describes his work in the Mines Rescue Service, particularly the Cortonwood disaster of 1961, and his progression to becoming an official, until having to accept redundancy in the summer of 1985. Cadeby finally closed towards the end of 1986.

"It was an eerie place because of the terrible disaster that had happened."

"After twelve months Jack [Hall, a Cadeby under-manager] moved me on. He made me the new mine air and dust sampler, in the safety department, which was a responsible job for a sixteen-year-old. Joe Humphries was the safety officer, a really fit man. He showed me what to do all over Cadeby Colliery. Every roadway had to be sampled for coal-dust each month. This included some of the old worked- out areas. On the Tuesday morning he told me that I would be going around the old South District the next day. No one had worked there since the 1912 disaster, apart from during World War Two when a little coal was worked, but away from the disaster area.

I had to take a tube similar to a test tube – for full analysis – and we went down No. 14 Stopping and shoved this long rubber pipe in (the old roadway had been stopped off) to take a sample. I carried Winchester bottles which each held three pints and we went up on the West Level and then to the South Plane Top – and there we got undressed and went down the South Return, bent double all the time. I had a cap lamp and Joe carried an oil lamp. Every Tuesday, for years, we did the same. It was an eerie place because of the terrible disaster that had happened. I can always remember one Tuesday we got to the South Plane and were about to get dressed when Joe told me that he had forgotten a pump, so he asked me to go back for it, alone. I set off and nearly got to 14's and then saw what I thought was a light but there was no one else down there. I wondered about ghosts. You could see names chalked where bodies had been found and deputies' initials and dates, chalked on roof girders. Sometimes you could find old tobacco pouches and newspapers in the packing areas, dating back to the early 1900s, even wooden tubs full of coal, left there from 1912. I looked again and the light was still there, so wondered what to do. It was the reflection of my cap light on black pitch on the old tram line girders which had been used in the roof area. I picked up the pump and ran a mile in, what seemed, less than a minute!

I had to sample every roadway and district in the pit, miles and miles of them but I got into it and blokes would stash me sampling equipment so that I could pick them up later.

I went into the Mines Rescue Service when I was twenty-one and remained until compulsory retirement, at forty-five, in 1977. The most memorable incident, early on, was to Shireoaks, dealing with a fire but the next one was at Cortonwood, in 1961, when several men were killed. I had been on afternoons that day. There had been an inrush of gas. The *Swallow Wood seam* was liable to pockets of gas but this one was so big it filled all the seam and these chaps were gassed. We were about to go to bed when I got the call. We went underground about 12.30 pm, wearing breathing apparatus. There was a lot of gas, even in an airlock at

Jeff Crabtree (second right) at the Cortonwood disaster of 1961. Jeff Crabtree

No. 2 shaft on the surface. None of the bodies had come out. The Cortonwood rescue team had done a survey first. We retrieved one body, a big chap called Bob Arnott, found dead on a Panza chain. The seam was only 2 foot 6 inches high, so it took two hours to get him off. There were some more dead further away but we had used up most of our Proto oxygen. We stayed at the fresh air base on standby until another team took us off. It was 8 am when we came out. Later I went on numerous fires at places such as Maltby and Silverwood and finished up as Captain of the Cadeby team. We trained at Rotherham Mines Rescue Station. Our fitness was tested each year.

My best friend at that time was Geoff Trout who was the ventilation officer. He wanted to do his coalface training so he could go as an official, but the manager would not let him go. He left and went to Denaby Main, so I got the ventilation officer's job. The money wasn't much but it was a job to get progression. I then did six months face training and then went into the *Haigh Moor seam*, higher up the shaft, and did two years until going on the staff as a shot-firer and deputy. I progressed to be an overman. I had a lot of responsibility, involved with production and linked with the under-manager and manager. On nights I was for all intents and purposes in charge of the pit. A good official has to be able to organise the work well and have good eyes to know what needs doing. You also have to be able to handle men. I always involved everybody. I gave the men an hour's overtime for a big job and got them together in the conference room to discuss the job; and also asked for their suggestions. This is much better than ordering people about. I treated the men as my equal and got a lot of respect as a result.

I retired on 13 July 1985, made redundant, on my 53rd birthday. The pit went into review after the strike and closed in December 1986. I was pushed into something that I did not want to do. On my last day I was on nights but spent the time in coal control. That was it, no presentation or anything but I will always remember being presented with a miniature oil lamp by Derek Ezra at the annual mines rescue dinner and dance, for twenty years in the service. He told me that I was a credit to the industry.

I have enjoyed my mining life, all my friends, and I would do the same again. Even if you were in management you had the same feeling of looking after each other, watching each others' back in case of an accident."

(40) Jeffrey Arthur Poar
(NCB Photographer)
Born: 4 January 1933
Place: Hirwaun, South Wales
Workplace base: Coal House, Doncaster
NCB work: c.1973 to 1989 (c.16 years)

What makes a good mining photographer? Having the right kind of equipment and, of course, access to pits certainly helps but I have no doubt that what makes Jeff Poar's work so outstanding was the rapport that he had with the miners and the great affection that he always had towards them. Jeff came from a Welsh mining background. His father, Thomas, worked at Tower Colliery from the age of thirteen and his Uncles were also pitmen. When Jeff left school (by which time the family had moved to the Midlands) he found employment in marine engineering but soon joined the RAF, eventually qualifying as a sergeant technician. Following a spell in a Birmingham factory, he returned to the

Jeff Poar with some of his photographic equipment, on an assignment at Kellingley. Jeff Poar

Air Force, and completed twenty-five years service. The following extracts from his interview start when Jeff talks about his first appointment with the National Coal Board. During the course of his work he visited many Yorkshire collieries, including the new Selby Complex, and also photographed miners in social and leisure situations. He was made redundant in 1989, and only given a few days to clear his desk.

"I used to get up in a morning and could not wait to get to work ..."

"My next main job [after RAF service] was working for the National Coal Board at Coal House, Doncaster, as a photographer. It was pure luck. I went there as a chauffeur. It was great. They employed four chauffeurs, and we were used to carry the managers and VIPs. There were also odd jobs, driving a van. I did this for eighteenth months and then a job in Public Relations came up. It was to assist the regional photographer by doing all his dark room work. I was a technician and an assistant to Bill Devey who was a smashing bloke. We got on very well together and never had a cross word. I had a good background as an amateur photographer and had been a member and chairman of various photographic clubs. Photography was a keen hobby of mine. When I first went for the job I was given a practical test and managed it straight away.

When Selby was being developed Bill needed a lot more help and I became his assistant, promoted to deputy Regional Photographer.

Our assignments were very varied. It was a newspaper-type of job really, but there was a great deal of underground work which was 'news breaking' rather than accidents, so the whole job was photographing people within the total environment of coalmining. The shots we took were used in magazines and newspapers such as *Coal News*. General newspapers also made plenty of use of our photographs as their staff photographers had not got the know-how and access to underground.

Bill was able to concentrate on picture taking when I was with him. I saw to the lighting and set things up. It was a great partnership. We always went down together. The flash was

Jeff Poar has produced many superb mining photographs. Here is a marvellous example from Emley Moor Colliery, dating from 1983. Jeff Poar

encircled in a one-inch steel case and weighed 14lbs, a massive piece of equipment which I carried on my shoulder and held in position for Bill. When I got promoted I had jobs to do on my own as well but we shared our assignments. If there were any record breakers or new equipment going underground then we would get involved. The main features were the miners. They were fantastic people. We used to have some banter with them and some of them would say that they wanted paying for having their photograph taken. It was all good fun and they soon came round, we had jokes and a good laugh. It was just what was needed for a good picture. Some of the men would even help me carry my equipment!

At Emley Moor Colliery I took some photographs in a very shallow seam, showing a man [Reuben Kenworthy] working on his side, getting coal with a pick in the old fashioned way. I had to crawl on my belly, there was hardly any height for the camera and helmet. The man was a wonderful fellow. They wanted to move him out of the seam which was getting more and more shallow, only about eighteen inches or even less, but he could not work in a three or four foot face. He said that he could not kneel and get coal as he was so used to working on his side in the old way.

The miners liked to take the mickey and there are many funny stories. Here's one that a deputy told me. Lord Robens (NCB Chairman) was due to visit Manton Colliery (Notts) so he

The Duchess of Kent, captured by the lens of Jeff Poar. Jeff Poar

told a [coal-cutting] machinist to smarten himself up for the VIP visit. Manton was a hot and dirty pit and the man usually just wore 'knicks' to work in. He also told him to take some water with him so he could have a good wash before Robens arrived. Well, when his lordship got there the man was lily-white clean and was wearing a pair of pink bloomers, with elastic up to his chest and elastic down to his knees! Robens never blinked an eyelid!

I took photographs of many VIPs. The best one was the Duchess of Kent. She was absolutely fabulous. We were making our way towards the face and Bill Devey was in front and I was following, my flash over my shoulder, and we got out at the gob [waste area] when, suddenly, she turned on her heels and made her way back to the face. We wondered what was going on. She tapped a miner who was close to Bill on his shoulder and said, 'Oh, by the way, who does your washing?' I thought that was a great thing to say, not expected from royalty but she was a lovely Yorkshire lass and so well liked. We photographed the Prince of Wales at Silverwood. We had to get in there quick because of his security and could not follow him all the time. Then there was Margaret Thatcher at Selby. She spoke to us and seemed interested and asked questions as she always did but I'm not one of her fans.

A great shearer at rest in a Yorkshire pit: another one of Jeff Poar's excellent underground photographs. Jeff Poar

I met Derek Ezra [NCB Chairman] on several occasions. He was one of the nicest people. He was always so interested, and a perfect gentleman – always well informed, having an answer to every question.

I also took photographs of the NUM leaders, especially at the miners' demonstrations. I remember on one occasion Arthur Scargill pointed his finger at me from the platform – or at least it seemed to be in my direction – and referred to the Fascist Tory press. He must have thought I was a photographer from the *Sun*! I made a point of putting him right when I met him again. The galas and demonstrations were always wonderful occasions.

I used to get up in a morning and could not wait to get to work as it was so varied and interesting. It was such an enjoyable job for me.

It was so sad to see the pits closing after the 84/85 strike. I remember travelling to Silverwood pit for an assignment in 1985 and went through Edlington where Yorkshire Main was situated. The pit had closed and by the time I returned, a few hours later, the pit-headgear had been demolished. It was as if they wanted to clear the landscape of mining as quickly as possible, to clear mining from people's memories. No one should ever forget the miners."

(41) Alex [Alexander Danforth] Carey

Born: 28 November 1933
Place: Mexborough
Pits: Hickleton Main; Goldthorpe Highgate; Hickleton; Brodsworth Main
Mining Experience: c.1949–1965; c.1973–1981 (c. 24 years)
Age at interview: 71

Alexander Carey in his Goldthorpe home, 25 February 2004. The author

When talking to Alex Carey about his early life it was clear that he continued to have fond memories of his great aunt and uncle, Charles [a collier] and Edith Troop, who brought him up in the mining village of Thurnscoe. In the following extracts Alex describes in useful detail aspects of his mining experiences, particularly at Hickleton Main. His memories include two sad occasions when one man was killed in a pony accident and another in a roof fall. At Goldthorpe Highgate Alex developed problems with his knees, a common occupational problem for miners, and left the industry for several years. Missing his workmates, he retrained at Markham and found employment at Brodsworth where he trained face-workers. Alex had to retire following an unexpected illness but, despite some rough times, remembers his mining life with a great deal of affection.

"You had to get down on your knees to dig in."

"I attended Thurnscoe Hill schools and was one of the first pupils to leave when the age was changed to fifteen, in 1949. We were all expected to go down the pit. The teachers arranged for us to have pit visits, so that we could have a look around the surface and underground. I walked down to see Mr Goldthorpe, the training officer at Hickleton, and got signed on. I was there for a week and then did six months training at Markham Main, Armthorpe.

It was exciting going down the first few times. When the men from the Ukraine came to work at Hickleton [from 1947] many of them did not like the ride down the shaft. They came over because of the shortage of labour after the war. Some of them stayed in a camp near Mexborough Hospital and others stayed at an old army camp at Hickleton.

I worked at the pit-bottom and was running coal off a slant. The chair came down with three empties and three full tubs would go on. You had to be careful, otherwise the tubs would fall into the shaft sump but they could be got out with chains. I had to catch the tubs on lockers.

When I was seventeen I went out into the districts because you could then get a bit of overtime. It was easier because at the pit-bottom you were at it all the time, as soon as the chair started riding the coal. A man on the districts, because the was no paddy to ride, had to walk a mile or two to get there but you were not 'working' when you were walking.

I moved to work at Goldthorpe Highgate pit between 1951–53 as I had a rupture developed from lifting at Hickleton. At Highgate I was driving a belt, keeping everything clear. It was all heading work there.

I went back to Hickleton, on the haulage, and it was a timber job, supplying to the coalfaces with tubs of wedges which we called lids, and props and bars. We would have a horse if we were lucky. My horses were called Fox and Jolly but I remember a horse called Masher [a white horse] which killed a man. He went wild and ran him into a man-hole, kicking him with its back legs. But Masher continued in service. A Ukrainian called Frank took him over and did a wonderful job. One day I was told to collect a horse from the stable [Masher] and take tubs of lids to the face but I did not know anything about pony driving. I went to open a door and pulled the horse to the front but he turned round and set off back – about three miles – to the pit-bottom. This happened three times! I had not hooked the horse back on to the tub. I was knackered when I had finished. The deputy laughed.

I then went into the coal. There was a three-year waiting list as it meant more money. At first I worked alongside a more experienced man. He would say to me, we'll we have eight pans here, eighteen yards of coal to fill-off and, when you went to it, it had been cut by the machines and fired after the borers had bored holes in your stint. You had to get down on your knees to dig in. I used a pick, a shovel and a 7 lb hammer. After shot-firing it was rare for all the coal to fall so you cleared up first and then started. The face about four foot high in the *Parkgate seam*, then I moved to the *Low Main Seam* where it was lower, so you could be working in two foot six or as low as eighteen inch. You would come on to the face when the shot-firers had done or the cutter men had cut it all and all the dust from the cutting would be heaped up. You would stand at the side of the pans and dig in until a little 'pog' [a hole in the coal made so as to let you in] was taken out and then get in there and start shovelling and throwing the coal on to the belt. All along the stint you would clear your way. In about 1955 I was getting just £5–6 per shift which made it hard to manage when you were just married.

I remember one bad accident when I was training. I was with a man in the waste. We were drawing props off and using chocks in the old way. They were steel props with Ridley bars. In the

Parkgate the roof had an eighteen inch cockle bed [hard black rock containing fossils]. A large lump came down from the roof, about six foot six inches long, eighteen inches thick and twenty-four inches wide and landed, with a support bar, on his legs. No one could get him out and they tried really hard. He died. I was twenty-one.

In the *Parkgate* it was always hot so you just wore your belt and if you were in the low part you would be in water. The man at the back of the last pan would be wearing wellingtons and a belt, no knickers, and he would hang his lamp up because there were no cap lamps at Hickleton. We had bucket lamps, weighing 10lbs. You hung your lamp between your legs or in your stint where you were working. You got used to the light and there would be a light in the next stint and so on, making a row of lights."

(42) George Rankin

Born: 4 July 1937
Place: Main Street, Bellshill, Lanarkshire, Scotland
Pits: Devon & Brucefield Colliery (Scotland); Markham Main (Armthorpe, Yorks)
Mining Experience: 1952–1989 (37 years)
Age at interview: 67

Several of the big and modern Doncaster area pits employed a good number of Scottish men, miners who had previously had had considerable skills and experience in more traditional and contrasting working environments. I met George Rankin, a former Markham Main man, at the Doncaster Local History Fair in September 2004. We got chatting about family history and Scottish and English mining terms, and he was kind enough to allow me to interview him. In this extract George, firstly, describes his Lanarkshire family background and his early working

Ex- Markham deputy George Rankin, proud of his Scottish roots, displays a Robbie Burns commemorative plate. The author

life in Clackmannanshire. He then talks about his move to Markham, his work there, including 'deputying' and, lastly, his memories of national strikes. George told me that he enjoyed Markham where it was 'a different challenge everyday', unlike his subsequent part-time work with a major food retailer.

"Markham was a colossal difference to the Scottish pits I had worked in."

"I was born at Bellshill, Lanarkshire in the central industrial belt of Scotland, about eight miles from Glasgow. I had two brothers and two sisters. My father, also called George, was a miner from the age of fourteen, working at several local pits. He suffered a broken leg and many cuts due to mining. On one occasion, when I was six years old, he came home with a bad cut on his leg, and was helped by his friend, David Grady, who started cleaning the wound. Mary, my mother, got a bent needle and some thread and David stitched the wound. To have a doctor would have cost a shilling which we could not afford.

I left school on a Friday, on my fifteenth birthday. I wanted to be a marine engineer but a new rule was brought out by the NCB whereby you could get a full year's holiday pay if you worked at the pit a fortnight before your holiday – so my Dad went to Stirling Arcade and bought me second-hand boots, overalls and a snap tin (which we call a piece tin) and off I went to the pit [Devon Colliery] on the Saturday morning. My dad could not wait for me to start, all for the £12 holiday pay. I got about £2.18s a week after stoppages. I remember getting to the pit for 6 am when I was given my tally number and waited at the top of the gangway. The pit-top gaffer, Steve Snadden, told me to go to the side of the shaft and I was to pull the full hutches [tubs] off the cage when they came up. I only did that for half a day when I was then told to see Rab Scobbie and learn how to mend the tubs. On the Monday Rab told me that I could put the tubs on, underground. It was about 100 fathoms deep but not on the level. Later, when the coal came off the belts, I filled the coal into the tubs. Later I was sent to Muircockhall, Dunfermline, for my official training which you had to have before working underground, though I had already worked underground! I came top out of over a hundred lads and was presented with a pen by John Gregson, the famous actor, who starred in the film about the Knockshinnock (Ayreshire) mine disaster, called *The Brave Don't Cry*.

I went to coalface training with my Dad at Brucefield. He taught me 'stripping' [filling]. After that I went back to the Devon pit and did what was called 'brushing' [ripping]. Then I did some 'packing' and 'putting', placing waste material in the gob which we called the 'cundy'. The packs were to slow the downward trend of the roof. My training certificate, when it was all done, stated my name as 'George Rankin', the stripper was George Rankin (my father), the safety officer was 'George Rankin' (my Uncle), so it was a family business! The faces varied from two and a half to five feet but they were very wet. They supplied you with oilskins but these were too uncomfortable to wear, so we ended up with arthritis.

I stayed at Devon colliery after my training for about a year and transferred to Brucefield, six miles towards Clackmannanshire. It was a drift mine, a small shallow mine where everyone knew each other, even the manager referred to us on first-name terms. It was cold and old fashioned. We only had a twelve inch Sampson coal-cutter, plus haulage, to take the coal to the pit-top. It was pick and shovel work.

I left in 1957 to come to Doncaster and got a job at Markham Main where my brother-in-law worked. He put me up at his house until Dorothy and I got married. I sent a letter from Clackmannan to the Head of the Secretariat, at the NCB and they told me when I could start and what shift I was on. On the Monday I saw the manager, Tom Cooper, [who] looked at me and said, 'Start tomorrow, on day shift.' He told me that I would be on the 'Nobbin' which meant when the miners were taking the coal out, to get the machine out, they had to have everything all flat and nice and tidy. There were three or four of us. If you finished early you filled a stint off, to reduce the [number of] men who would be filling on the next shift. Markham was a colossal difference to the Scottish pits I had worked in. When I came off the cage on my first shift I bent back and looked up … I had never seen a pit-bottom so big. Normally I was used to a pit-bottom that only just cleared your head.

I was treated OK [by the local men] but had my leg pulled a bit. After a few weeks I gave as good as I got. There were other Scottish men there but I was friends with anyone, not just the Scottish lads.

I came off the Nobbin and went on to coal filling for a long time, and did some ripping. In about 1968 the overman, Ralph Cutts, came round one day shift and asked me I fancied becoming a deputy. I said 'No' but later, after talking about it with Dorothy, I decided to go ahead and I was interviewed and qualified, in February 1972.

Being a deputy was strange to begin with because you had worked alongside the men and suddenly I was telling them what to do, responsible for their health, safety and welfare. What makes a good

Detail from the commemorative pulley wheel at Armthorpe, Doncaster, in memory of the eighty-seven miners who were killed at Markham Main and the men and women who worked there. The author

deputy is fairness and honesty – and not to hold any grudges. When I left the pit the men who worked for me were good to me and my wife. I worked with a good team.

I did not get any money during the 1972 strike as I had only just signed over as a deputy. I was in limbo. Bill Abbiss, the Union delegate, gave me some money every week and I paid it back when the strike was over. Picketing wasn't too bad in the 1970s but was more prominent in the 1984/85 strike. Most of the lads were brilliant, they caused no trouble but I must say the police did, not so much from South Yorkshire but from the Metropolitan force. My friend, Jimmy Webster, took photographs from his bedroom window, showing the police running riot. We reported to the pit gates each day, signed the book, then went back home. The only time that we went down was about half way into the strike when there was a fire, so went down, along with some of the men, but that was exceptional and was sanctioned by the NUM and NACODS. As soon as the fire was over and sealed off the men were back on strike. Markham was out for a year and a week. There was a march back when deputies marched back with the men. Generally, there was no ill feeling afterwards between the deputies and the men, there was good rapport;but there was bad feeling with the scabs and most of them left the pit. Production was good after the strike and the pit was in remarkably good condition. The management, though, were more powerful than ever. What they said had to be done and it was never the same again."

(43) Mick Carter

Born: March 1943
Place: Nottingham
Pits: Cortonwood; Silverwood
Mining experience: c1966–1993 (27 years)
Age at interview: 60

As the Union Delegate for Cortonwood Colliery it was understandable that Mick Carter came to public prominence during the 1984–85 miners' strike. It was the announcement of the pit's closure that was generally regarded as the spark that ignited the dispute. Thus, Mick was often in demand by the media. Almost twenty years later he was approached once again by television companies, radio and the press, asking him for his recollections and opinions due to the widespread interest in the impending anniversary of the strike.

Mick Carter, NUM Cortonwood delegate during the 1984/85 miners' strike. Michelle Carter

Despite his ill-health he had no hesitation in granting my request to meet and interview him in his Brampton home, in November 2003.

Mick left Brampton Secondary Modern at the age of fifteen. His first settled job was as an apprentice fitter at Newton Chambers, Chapeltown where he became interested and active in trade union affairs. He started work at Cortonwood in 1966 and continued with his union activities at local level, also developing a detailed knowledge of the Mines & Quarries Act which he regarded as 'the Bible', helping him towards election as a Union Mines Inspector prior to the introduction of safety committees. Mick stayed at Cortonwood until the pit closed in November 1985 when he transferred to Silverwood, which he described to me as the most unhappiest time of his working life, keeping his dignity despite 'silent victimisation'. After Silverwood Mick was a student of Sociology and Social Policy at York University, completing his degree in 2000 and, but for his illness, would have started a doctorate and a period of teaching.

I will never forget my interview with Mick Carter, who spoke with insight and honesty about the most momentous year in modern working class history.

"… it was a smack in the gob when news came through [that Cortonwood was to close].*"*

"In September [1983] Elsecar closed and all those [men] over fifty were transferred to Cortonwood. They were told not to panic as we had five years coal left. In October or November we started an overtime ban, nothing to do with wages, which had been voted on as a means of protest … the wording was against closing any pit or unit on economic grounds. From the overtime ban starting, all of a sudden lorries stopped coming into the yard, trains stopped and the stock pile was getting bigger – there was no coal going out, so I knew something was in the wind. They told us that we had 'lost the markets' but our coal was the finest in Britain but that it as 'too good' … there was a lot of suspicion, but it was a real smack in the gob when news came through to us [that Cortonwood was to close].

During the overtime ban the tactics used by the Coal Board changed entirely to what had happened before. For example, in 1972, even before the strike started, we were getting power cuts every hour for days. There were no lights in Blackpool. When we went on the overtime ban they said that it was not affecting production. A load of balls! Most pits were losing production, especially on Mondays. Some pits were being laid off for days on end. Kellingley was laid off for two weeks. Totally different tactics … they tried all that they could to rub the lads up but no one was biting.

Then it happened – at Cortonwood. It could have been Wath, any pit of the 206 and the result would have been the bloody same. It was not a case of being left wing. It was the way it was done. I was told [the news], as Branch Delegate. I had been in a meeting with the manager on the Thursday. A new face was almost ready to go into production and plans were for it to go into full production on 12 March. We were sorting the final manpower list. We were full of hope because we knew that this new face was better.

I stopped at the pit for half an hour or so and when I was walking up the pit lane Arnie Young, our Area Agent, came down in his car and honked his horn at me. He did not pick me up, the bugger! I walked back and he was stood outside the Union Office. That's when he told me. He had just come from a quarterly meeting of the Area, with news that we were shutting on 5 April. These meetings were held to go through every pit and look at present and future production, regular meetings, nothing suspicious and the Union was always represented. Arnie said that Gregory [Area Director] had said … in open meeting … that he would not refer to Cortonwood until the last [pits were usually evaluated alphabetically] and would not say why when asked. When pushed he then said that he had made a decision that Cortonwood would cease production on 5 April, on economic grounds.

Historic NUM notice announcing meetings to be held in the wake of the unexpected news of the imminent closure of Cortonwood Colliery, March 1983. Michelle Carter

What do you do? You are on an overtime ban, based on any action taken on closures on economic grounds. Safety factors were involved in previous closures. Geological problems are difficult to argue against. But we knew we had five years left. The new faces had cost millions to develop. I put the question to him on live TV and he admitted it. He had been given instructions that he had got to cut production by a certain amount and the projected production [figures] over the next twelve months [by closing Cortonwood] 'fitted' his [target] figure. In five years you can plan and prepare for another job but five weeks' notice left us hopeless.

On Monday, 5 March, we took the action, or the men did. We were out. An emergency Council meeting was called and at tea-time we went to Silverwood for an emergency panel meeting. I gave a report as to why we were on strike and asked for support. They decided to come out from the night shift. We heard that the Doncaster Area had done the same. All four Areas held panel meetings that day. Barnsley and North Yorkshire decided to work for another week and also the [Area] Workshops. This gave them time to hold Branch meetings and get the men's support. Straight away we set a picket up at the lane end. We made a seminal mistake as a union, in the first week of the strike, 15 March, when David Jones was killed. We came out on the 5th … We were quite content to give Barnsley and North Yorkshire a week's grace to consult democratically with their membership but we were not prepared to give Notingham the same grace. This was a big mistake. I believe that if Nottingham had had the ballot they were screaming for, give them two weeks, it would not have made any difference to them. They would not have struck. Nottingham's history made it predictable. They were then determined not to join the strike when Doncaster and Hatfield went down. Everything built up from that. You can't re-write history, lad. If Notts had decided to come out the strike would not have lasted. They had the propaganda that undermined everything. They believed the false promises … the Union of Dopey Miners (UDM) … but as soon as the strike was over and their pits were beginning to be shut and they were screaming foul. That's how thick they were.There were no lengths that the government would not go to get the miners down.

We were prisoners in our own village. Phones were tapped. It was obvious. As soon as you set foot outside you were followed; and that happened elsewhere. And yet, at the Notts NUM headquarters, at Berry Hill, Mansfield, owned by the NUM, two guys walked in and turfed out Henry Richardson and Chadburn, Area President and Secretary and it was taken over by the UDM – with the police helping them! Now, could you believe that? We would have been put in Lincoln nick if we had tried to take over the Yorkshire NUM offices in Barnsley!

I bet the police had every registration within three weeks of the strike. They had names and addresses from Swansea. It was a feather in their cap if they [the pickets] got to a destination but they often got turned back. They would compete against each other to get there first or stay the longest.

One of the most important documents that appeared was the Monopolies and Mergers Report of 1980. Two volumes. I've got it. She's [the report author] actually put blank pages in

Mick Carter gestures towards Cortonwood Colliery, as if to say 'this is our pit for our community' – as previously agreed by the NCB. John Davies/Daily Mirror

it. It says in the preface that certain parts of the report had been omitted as they were 'politically sensitive'. It just happened to be on the section on colliery finances. It lists every pit in a profitable league, from the most profitable to the least profitable and out of the 206 pits at the time Cortonwood was No 45, so if they were talking about shutting the pit on economic grounds what about all the others? That's why we knew it was a political move.

It was only a few years ago that the BBC admitted that they had reversed the film footage [at Orgreave]. But the damage was done when it went on the news. People have a strong belief in television, even more than newspapers. That was one of the worst crimes of the strike. Nobody could believe me when I addressed meetings. We were 'thugs'. It altered public opinion … Orgreave was a solitary lesson. Police brought in all the reinforcements and, to this day, I have no trust in the police. No respect. Bringing in the Met and other forces caused great distress.

The winter was difficult. One of the biggest problems was trying to get some assistance. We were fortunate … we had twinning arrangements, for example with the River Don Works at Sheffield. We got £200 a week off them, for food. People did not starve. That was seen to, even if they were from another pit we accommodated them. Christmas was awkward because of the kids, so a lot of women worked hard to collect money to buy toys but there was real hardship, it was getting very difficult.

It never seemed to change for me, from one week to the next. Not many men went back here. It was disheartening but inevitable. No matter how long or whatever cost there were no lengths that the Government would go to ensure that they crucified us. It started [the return to work] as a trickle and became a flood. It was not easy calling the strike off when you have sacrificed such a lot but we all said we went back with our heads high. High heads but a dead heart.

It was strange going back to work because of the attitudes. There was a lot of bitterness between the officials as they had got paid during the strike and this lasted for some time. And we could not find out who had scabbed – they knew who they were but we did not need to be told. They were protected to some extent. Men would not work with them.

I always got on well with Arthur Scargill. Agreed with just about everything he said. He was very much misunderstood and maligned. People that do not know him get the impression he is an

Mick Carter's daughter, Michelle, displays an oil painting of her father. The author

abrasive character, a red ragger etc. You could guarantee that when he was Area President if a pit came out they would get a phone call from Barnsley: 'Get them back, you can't talk until you get them back'. The public might have thought he would say,'Keep them out'. He was not that kind of guy at all. A strike, to Arthur, was always a last resort. I did not agree with him on some things but he was true to his job … his [Arthur's] face would be as long as a cow's arse if he got knocked back, but that same night on *Calendar* when he was speaking you could not know he had been nearly in tears early on in the day. He was elected to give the view of the members. That's what he did, always put forward the view that had been decided at a meeting.

Margaret Thatcher? Well, bless her … She had got it in for the miners. Revenge for Ted Heath. That's why MacGregor was brought in. We had strong suspicions after what he had done to the steel industry. It was a case of where and when.**"**

(44) Stuart Woodlock

Born: 25 May 1944
Place: Hyde Terrace, Leeds
Pits: Allerton Bywater; North Yorkshire Area Workshops (Allerton Bywater); Ledston Luck
Mine Engineering: Dosco Engineering; Exchem Mining
Mining experience: c.1959–2003 (44 years)
Age at interview: 61

It was fascinating meeting Stuart Woodlock because of his extensive experience of mining in many locations; and also because he had only been retired from the industry for a few months. The son of an engine man (George Woodlock) who was a winder at Glass Houghton and Kellingley collieries, Stuart's first job was at a Castleton glassworks but the pull of mining, with better pay and working with former school friends, was irrestible. In the following extracts we hear about his early experience as a 'hopper lad' at Allerton Bywater Colliery, and his continued interest in the trade of 'fitting', working underground,

Stuart Woodlock and his grandson, Allerton Bywater, Castleford, 29 April 2004. Stuart had only recently retired from the mining industry. The author

repairing and installing machinery. His skills were certainly in demand when he moved to the Area Workshops where he gained further experience working at many Yorkshire pits. A subsequent spell at Ledston Luck was the prelude to engineering appointments with the Dosco and Exchem companies, experience which included work overseas. In particular, Stuart became well-known for installation and advice relating to roof-bolting and the use of a variety of modern mining technologies.

"I decided to move to Allerton Bywater, signed on by Dick Beresford, a grand fellow. At seventeen I was too old to do the six months training but too young to do twenty days underground training at Whitwood pit, so I worked as a hopper lad on the washery. The hoppers filled up with singles, doubles, trebles, smalls ... men lowered their wagons underneath and I opened the hoppers, filling the wagons with the coal. On my eighteenth birthday the boss fitter, Billy Cowell, wanted me to stay there as a young fitter but I wanted to join the underground fitters, so went to Whitwood for my training. There were training galleries for the basics such as ripping, packing, filling etc and visits to working faces. They had a Meco, the power-loading machine of the day, as well as hand-filling faces. I went under the ripping on one of the hand-filling faces and saw Kenny Pass and other lads filling and was mesmerised by these shiny black fellas shovelling coal in the warm conditions.

On my first day back at Allerton Bywater the overman, Walter 'Snowy' Portman, sent me with an old fellow, 'Fagga' Taylor, drilling holes in rings for the fishplates. I really wanted to go with the fitters. Next day he told me to go down the Silkstone with 'Pop Oyle' Dick and 'Gawk' Wainwright, cleaning up, shovelling up on the blind side of the *Silkstone* 15's belt. I was shovelling like a collier. I still wanted to be among the fitters, so on the next day I went with Jackie Bratt's team in the *Flockton* [Seam]. I was a fitter's lad. On the first shift he sent me with a great guy, Les Prince, and we went in the *Flockton*, on a Meco face. I knew from then on that fitting was the job for me, working on the faces. I qualified as a grade 1 fitter in 1965.

Of all the pits that I have worked Allerton Bywater was was the best. Everybody seemed to fit hand in glove with each other and everything was good. Even in adverse conditions you could have a laugh and a joke, especially down the *Haigh Moor*. I spend a lot time on Haigh Moor 8's trepanner face. The *Flockton Thin* was a nice seam. It was cool but not wet. In contrast, the *Silkstone*, much deeper, burnt my face and there was more dust. I worked on one *Silkstone* face, 17's, a plough face, no more than two foot high. It was a nightmare repairing there. It eventually closed up from the middle, over a 200 yard length. I remember Jackie Bratt, the boss fitter, sending me down one night to uncouple the pans in the middle of the face ... I crawled there and shone my lights but decided to leave the pans ... I could not get any further so they had to pull off what they could.

I was at Allerton Bywater until 1967 and, having married a year earlier, wasn't happy about continuing working all the shifts, so I got a transfer to the Area Workshops on Newton Lane. As more pits got mechanised they did not have the experienced people to install and repair the new machines, so the Area would send a team. There may be a team of three or four of us sent to wherever was required, for example to Hatfield Main or Bentley or even Linby in Notts. Hatfield was a good pit, a nice pit but when you went down the shaft it stank of sulphur and the smell would stay with you all day. There were some good lads there, including Lol Madill. We worked on the chocks on the faces. Bentley was pretty warm and dusty when we were repairing chocks. Yorkshire Main at Edlington was a nightmare when I went there, installing Dosco machines. It was very hot and there were cooling systems in the roadsides to chill the air. Maltby was also a hot pit. Rossington could be a bit awkward, some good lads but they could be a law unto themselves. Brodsworth had huge chairs, capable of transporting over 200 men per ride. At Barnburgh the showers were excellent, the water always lovely and soft with big shower heads. When I was at Area I also spent time at Hickleton, installing Dosco machines.

Stuart Woodlock (extreme left) in Ackworth Colliery, working at the ripping lip in the Silkstone seam. *Sitting next to Stuart is John Cairns and on the extreme right is colliery Deputy Brian Newbould., December 1980.* Stuart Woodlock

I was earning good money in the Area and power loading was being introduced but more lads at their own pits had learned what to do with the new machines, so our work got less and I returned to the normal Area rate – but with a young family to keep decided, in about 1970, to transfer to Ledston Luck. It was a smashing little pit, not deep, and a family pit. I spent most of my time in the headings where they had just installed Dosco machines. I was suited to this work because of my ripping machine experience. I really liked it there but there could be a lot of water, making some jobs nasty. You could be caked in mud and it was cool.

Later, I was invited by Dosco for interview as one of their engineers and was successful, so I left the NCB but remained in the NUM. Most of my time was spent at the pits that I covered when working for the Area. The men at the pits treated me really well. Soon my boss asked how I would feel about travelling. I told him that I think that I would be able to handle it. I was sent to North Wales, Leicestershire, Lancashire and Scotland, staying in hotels until the job was done. The machinery was dispatched from Tuxford to the pits. I would go to see it, take it underground, build it and test it, and train the men, all part of the customer service.

Travelling included trips abroad, to Argentina in the hot English summer of 1976 but it was very cold there as I was working at the southern tip of the Andes. It was a twenty-five hour

*Stuart Woodlock – with colliery overman Stuart Beaumont –
demonstrating roof bolting in Houghton Main, March 1988.* Stuart Woodlock

flight and I was on my own. I got by with a little Spanish and some of the men there had a smattering of English. The country was in turmoil and was run by the military. The pits were driven into the side of the mountain and the underground situation was similar to ours in the UK. The rapport between the men and myself was very good. A lot of them travelled in each day from Chile, riding on open-topped lorries. Building the machines on the surface was difficult because it was dark until ten in the morning and then again by three in the afternoon, and the temperature could be 20–30 degrees below freezing. Everything was successful and the mine manager even presented me with a medal. I also travelled to Brazil for a brief assignment.

I saw a job advertised for a firm that became known as Exchem. It was far better pay and there was less travelling. I became involved in the introduction of roof bolting. I knew all the pits by now, even had checks waiting for me at each one. Once I had succeeded at one pit word would spread to the manager next door and he would ask me to come over. On some days I never took my work clothes off, servicing three pits in a single day, so was in demand. Roof bolting became more common, and I installed systems throughout Yorkshire, including the developing Selby Complex and even worked in Sardinia. The Mines Inspectorate were very wary at first and so were the unions but this was understandable until roof bolting was proved.

By the late 1980s Australian methods were introduced, and improved upon, and, after pit closures, I was still in demand since the remaining pits wanted to maximise their efficiency, using the most modern methods. I continued with Exchem through to April 2003 but, approaching sixty years old, I decided to retire while I was still healthy.

For years, from 1978 to 1995, I worked in conditions that you could not imagine and some faces where the lads worked were terrible; but generally, I've had a good mining life, with a great amount of variety and met a lot of good working lads."

(45) Peter Finnegan

Born: 9 September 1945
Place: County Armagh, Ireland
Pits: Manvers Main; Goldthorpe
Mining experience: c.1961–1974 (13 years)
Age at interview: 58

Peter Finnegan is well-known in the Bolton-on-Dearne area and elsewhere because of his many charity initiatives and campaigns, most notably in respect of children's hospices. A member of the Bolton Heritage Group, I interviewed him in the Dearne Valley Venture recording studio. He talked about his disadvantaged and remarkable childhood (which reminded me of the writings of David Pelzer) and coping with a speech impediment and dyslexia. In the extract we hear about Peter's memorable first day at work in the woodyard at the pit-top, his early work underground as a 'lines lad' [trainee surveyor], his clothes and equipment and progression to a variety of jobs. He concludes by recounting his personal decision to quite mining on health grounds.

Peter Finnegan with a collection of his mining tools and equipment, Bolton-upon-Dearne, 2004. The author

"I was like a little packhorse!"

"I came to live at Bolton-upon-Dearne in 1952 when I was seven years old. We got a pit house [59 Broadwater] in the 'Concrete Canyon' area. I had never seen a house before. We lived in a run down cattle shed on the Northern Ireland border. My father had abandoned us at an early age. I had never seen a bathroom, a sink or even a tap. Good Lord, we could not understand why water came from a tap as we had an old well or used a pump. Having a toilet was unbelievable. We washed in a half barrel.

My mother [Mary] died when I was fourteen. Father [Peter] was a brutal man. I was like a house slave. I scrubbed his shirts with soap and water, ironed them and cleaned the house and fed myself from left-over scraps of food. He spent money on drink, fags and gambling. I had the fastest legs in the village – running to the betting office. I had to fend for myself so at fifteen I started work at the pit. It was the only way to get a decent wage. I went to see Fred Smith, the training officer at Manvers Main and was set on in the woodyard on the pit-top. It was mid-September 1960. I remember my first day well as a man who worked down the *Haigh Moor seam* and had lost all his holiday money on the horses, had come back to the pit and thrown himself down the shaft.

The woodyard was the place where timbers were stacked and collected before they went down the pit. There were split bars, clog lumps that went under packs, crown bars and many others – and lids to go over the top of the props; and then there were metal rings. We would stack them all. This was before starting my underground training.

My first wage was £3 17s. I went home to my father with the packet unopened and put it on the table. He picked it up, opened it and chucked it back to me, saying, 'In this country you must give me £4. The board is £4, so go and find another 3s.' Mrs Stott took me away from my father just afterwards, and then Mrs Talbot, taking me in off the streets. I called her 'Ma'. She is now ninety-six. One day I had lemon cheese in my snap and told her it was great but then she gave me it everyday! I stayed with her until I got married. Having your snap underground, you just ate where you were working. The air might be stale and putrid. You were not supposed to bring your snap wrapped in paper as it was classed as contraband. You could not wash your hands after 'going to the toilet'. Life down the pit was not fit for humans. I once fetched a dudley full of milk but by the time I got into the district it was sour.

I was at Manvers Training Centre, a day at college and four days underground training in the *Meltonfield*. When I had done I had to go back to the woodyard as I was not old enough to work underground until I was sixteen.

When I went down officially I worked with Eddie Balance, a Wath man and an ex-

'Carry On Peter': this imaginative stunt, carried out over a thousand hours in a portaloo, was to protest against the lack of Government funding for children's hospices, and attracted international media interest. Bolton-upon-Dearne, 2004. The author

sergeant major who was a deputy and head surveyor. He was a great guy. He taught me to respect people there.

My first job was as a lines lad. Eddie would show people how to make the tunnels straight. He made sure that you measured up the workings and they went in the proper direction, using a dial. You had to be precise. On the first day we went into the North East District which we needed to keep in line but when we started we were telephoned to to go straight to the South East District as a man was seriously injured, so we had to measure up there. It was a guy I always respected … who lived near me in the Concrete Canyon, a lovely chap. He was crushed and killed on the first mechanised face. Our measurements were for the accident report. It was the saddest day of my life. Doing the linesman's job, I got to know every part of the pit.

I carried some right tackle with me when I was working. I wore a helmet, old trousers but no shirt or vest but had a belt for my battery, respirator, oil lamp, two powder bags (weighing

7lb each – you got extra money), bits for boring, a seven or eight pint dudley and a snap tin. I was like a little packhorse! but I ran to the district, didn't bother with the paddy mail, just wanted to get on with it.

I did ripping, hand-filling using a pick and shovel, pan-turning and back-ripping. I worked in a good team … The comradeship was superb.

In 1966 I was buried on the south-east face and my back was skinned raw. I went to work the next day but was sent home. I was off sick for six weeks.

I became a picket during the 1972 miners' strike. We went to Salmon Pastures, near Sheffield, a coal depot near Attercliffe. I fell down a chute, it was snowing and I must have gone unconscious since a day and a half went by before I went to hospital. My health was being affected by mining. I was coughing black phlegm up and my hearing was being affected by the noise. I tried moving to Goldthorpe but only for a few weeks, working on a button which didn't suit me so I decided to concentrate on running my own wholesale and retail business, leaving mining for good in 1974.

I missed the comradeship. You can not beat a miners. They would share their last crust of bread. You had to look out for each other."

(46) Michael Taylor
Born: 14 April 1946
Place: Chesnut Avenue, Kendray, Barnsley
Pits: Monk Bretton; Dodworth; Dodworth Redbrook; Barnsley Main; Goldthorpe
Mining experience: 1962–1968; 1974–1994 (26 years)
Age at interview: 58

Michael Taylor started work at Monk Bretton Colliery, where his father, Harry (see page 41) was a deputy. Straight from school (aged fifteen), he worked on the screens, in 1962. This was a time when there was considerable demand for young mining recruits but Michael was understandably disappointed when the pit closed six years later and he spent a few years out of the industry. Nevertheless, mining was part of Michael's life but his subsequent career was interrupted by more pit closures and transfers, and he ended it at Goldthorpe, the last working pit in the Barnsley area. Michael talked in some detail about his underground experiences at Monk Bretton, starting as a

Michael Taylor (right) with his late father, Harry Taylor, Kendray, 1 March 2004. The author

pony driver and 'learning the trade'; and there were also useful comments about his later work and the 1984/85 strike.

"I will never forget my first day filling."

"Going down the shaft at Monk Bretton took some getting used to. You could tell who was the winder as some days it went down really fast [and] your heart went in your stomach, which was not very good first thing on a Monday morning. My first job was pony driving, taking timber to the faces. We took several tubs at a time. The stableman was Lol Green. If you went back with a pony that was hurt it would not be long before he gave you a skelp round the lughole. I had a pony called Robin, another was called Duke and there was Jack. The men were hand-filling in the *Beamshaw* and *Winter seams*. The *Beamshaw* could not be sheared as it was too bad, a yard of muck always fell as the top did not hold. There were some runaways if the chain slipped when we were lashing on. I would go and see all the damage, usually the smashed tubs but the pony would be stood nearby. Once I helped carry one man out [of the pit] when his nervous pony was startled and stampeded over him, pulling the tram on top of him. He was badly shaken. It was high enough to ride but once my pony tripped and I went flying over its head. I got up fast in case it trampled on me! I did pony driving until I was eighteen.

I will never forget my first day filling. I got straight into it, working really fast but next to me was an old gentleman who was just working steady – he had filled off an hour before me! He always got a right shovel full. I was on my knees all the time, using a pick, square-faced, No 5 shovel, and a hammer for setting the timber: six foot bars and three foot six inch props. I was really tired that first day. I also did ripping, heading work and shearer driving. When you were in the market you could also be sent anywhere to work, including the waste [gob] or on a button, anything, that was going.

I used to go to Monk Bretton pit with my dad, riding on the back of his motorbike if we were on the same shift. I even worked under him when he was a deputy. There was no problem with that and he did not give me any favours!

I saw the training officer, George Marsden, at Dodworth Colliery, just after the 1974 strike, and got set on straight away. I was a face-worker. It was all mechanised, with shearers and I also went ripping but only stayed there six months when Redbrook was opened up. Redbrook was a little shaft pit which had an 'orange box' cage which, officially, held just six on the top deck and six on the bottom, though it could hold double on the way out! I got a regular job ripping on the maingate. It was a family pit. I got on really well, working with the younger lads.

I was on strike twelve months [1984–85]. It was devastating but I would never have gone back [ie 'scabbed']. I did some picketing with the North Gawber lads. I used to go to the Civic Hall for my dinner, thanks to the women there. I had two children still at school. We got £5 each for them from Social Security but there was nothing for me. We were told to march back with our heads held high but it felt degrading for us to finish. I would have stayed out longer. Afterwards, no one talked to the scabs. I would not work with them. The atmosphere was terrible. The management took advantage of the situation and did everything by the book.

When Redbrook shut, in December 1987, I went to Barnsley Main which had become part of Barrow Colliery. Again, I was on shearer faces and I did ripping and worked in headings, did everything. On one occasion in a heading it pinged all the rings, flattened them with the weight. I was involved in another accident too, on a face, in the chocks and on afters. We were walking down the tailgate and I felt dizzy and so did the others. It was gas. We turned around and shot back up the gate and were taken out and out in an ambulance. It was a big scare and filmed for *Calendar* [Yorkshire TV]. A spark could have blown the pit to

Former Barnsley Main Miner Michael Taylor displays a framed photograph of the colliery, signed by 'the last employees at the last coal mine to work in the Borough of Barnsley' and dated July 1991. The author

smithereens. A hole was found, blown through the floor, from which gas was escaping and coming up the tailgate.

Barnsley Main closed in 1991 so I moved to Goldthorpe. I wanted to give it another go and had heard good reports about wages there. It was a fantastic pit. The *Shafton seam* was very productive. Conditions were very good apart from the last face. We could not hold it, tried timbering every day but it was always flopping in. I had some narrow escapes. On shearer faces there was a chain for the coal and we had to set it to timber-up but we had to be wary of lumps coming down. It was easy to get injured. Sometimes it would sling a stone or piece of coal and this happened to me at Goldthorpe, splitting my nose open. I was taken to hospital and was off work for a while.

When Goldthorpe finished in 1994 I realised it was the end of my mining life as I did not want to travel all the way to Selby. I had had enough. I've enjoyed my mining life and miss the lads."

(47) Robert 'Bob' Taylor

Born: 15 January 1952
Place: Listerdale, Rotherham
Pits: New Stubbin; Cortonwood; Silverwood
Working experience: 1968–71 & 1979–1993 (17 years)
Age at interview: 52

Bob Taylor is one of the four striking miners featured in *Yorkshire's Flying Pickets* (Wharncliffe Books, 2003) based on the diary of former Silverwood miner Bruce Wilson. Bob has a keen interest in mining history and took part in the re-enactment of 'The Battle of Orgreave' filmed for Channel 4 on 17 June 2001. A Rawmarsh lad, Bob found employment at his local pit, New Stubbin, shortly after leaving school. Following training at Manvers and a variety of pit-top work Bob's first underground job was 'on the haulage', progressing to face training at the age of eighteen (at

Silverwood). A few years' work at the River Don steelworks, followed, prior to returning to mining, at Cortonwood Colliery, in 1979. This employment was interrupted, in March 1984, by the start of the miners' strike. Here, Bob describes some of his experiences in the year-long dispute. After the closure of Cortonwood he transferred to Silverwood which he described as 'like coming home', staying there until September 1993, shortly before the pit closed. He now works for the First Line Bus Company in Rotherham.

BobTaylor is rarely seen without his cap, in this case enhanced by miners' strike badges relating to the 1984/85 dispute. Rawmarsh, 2 March 2003. The author (Inset) *A Junior School photograph of Bob Taylor. Note the US-style crewcut.* Bob Taylor

"I felt betrayed by the closure announcement."

"We had had the overtime ban, leading up to the strike. I didn't really think the pit was at risk as older blokes were being transferred from Elsecar, which had shut, to us and we expected another five years of working life for the pit. The news of closure came out of the blue, especially to those who had just been transferred. There was a meeting at the parish hall at Brampton and I attended. I wanted to fight the pit closure. Mick Carter put his case for us. I felt betrayed by the closure announcement. We supported Mick's arguments to keep the pit open. It was our livelihood anyway. Everybody felt the same.

The strike started. A cabin was put together at the end of the pit lane, for pickets and was called the Alamo. We said we would fight to the last man, that's why it got its name. We all knew it would be the centre of attention of the media when the strike started. Cameras everywhere. I was on telly for a few seconds! I used to go there picketing a few times early on but I wanted to go with the flying pickets, preferring some action. I used to walk to Brampton from Rawmarsh where I lived. Someone told me to go over to the Baggin, Silverwood Miners' Welfare and have a word with their union man to see if I could go with them. I spoke to Granville Richardson, their union bloke, who put me in touch with Bruce Wilson and that's how it all started. There were a team of four of us to begin with and then Darren joined us. I was called 'Captain Bob'. It was all right, I enjoyed it.

We were in some right scrapes. We went to Orgreave a lot. Early on we would go to Nottingham in a morning, or try and get there, if we could get through the roadblocks and then come back, have our dinner at the Baggin and go to Orgreave in the afternoon. It was OK because you got £1 for going into Nottinghamshire and another £1 for Orgreave. Double time, kid! There were some really bad days, even before that Monday, 18 June when there were mass pickets from all over the country. It was frightening when the cavalry charged, on the fields and through the streets, all over the place. Even Jack Taylor ran faster than me – sparking clogs on that day!

At Pye Hill, Nottinghamshire, I got chased by about twenty-eight scabs, I daren't look round, I was on my own on a lane. Five of us had been going there all week, afternoon shift went in, went there again on Monday, there were four of us there, I was big then and not as fast as the other three, so by the time I had set off they all got off the bus. I heard one at the back of me shout, 'I'm going to have you, you little fat bastard!' I must have took a wrong turning as I was hiding behind this weeping willow and they missed me! I often have flashbacks about that, like a war veteran. If I had tripped and fallen down I might have been booted to death.

I never got into the situation where I was on the front line as I could have been suffocated, though you couldn't always guarantee it. We were in that position at Maltby, though. Silverwood got bad as well. You knew you were in a war zone when Kate Adie was there! She was reporting to television cameras just like any other battle.

At the end of the strike we did not even go in on the first day because of the Kent miners' presence, so we refused to cross picket lines. I didn't really want to go back. I went back in my car with me not living local, though I would have liked to have walked back with the banner.

I didn't find any of the police all right to us during the strike. the police were from all over, Manchester, Staffordshire, London. If it wasn't for the scabs we might have won, it would not have been such a long strike. The public figures that I did not like were Thatcher and MacGregor, and Leon Britton, the Home Office minister. Arthur Scargill was a good lad. I would have gone to the end of the world for him. He was right all the time. Right in what he said.

When I went back to work the atmosphere at the pit was just not the same. It wasn't same with the management either. A lot of deputies did not work and some gave their money up but others got paid. Working with scabs was a bad feeling. I worked with one bloke who had been placed on his own. I never realised he was a scab at first. We had to unload some big drums of oil. I got talking to him. He was from Elsecar and I asked how one of the lads was getting on – one who crossed the picket line and had a nervous breakdown, so I asked about him. In next breath he told me that he had gone to work. He told me that he was in debt, by £2,000 but I walked off and left him to unload it on his own. I went to another level.

When Cortonwood closed, in November 1985, I got transferred to Silverwood which was like going home, to my local pit. I started working on the transfer point, on the button, watching belts. I finished in September 1993, not long before the pit closed, though I did not know that. I was placed in an awkward position due to rumours that the redundancy situation might be changed so I decided to call it a day. I did not want to finish, though. There was no real choice."

Bob Taylor, flanked by two former Silverwood mates, Bruce Wilson (left) and Granville Richardson, with the Silverwood NUM banner in the background. Rotherham Central Library and Arts Centre, April 2004. The author

Glossary

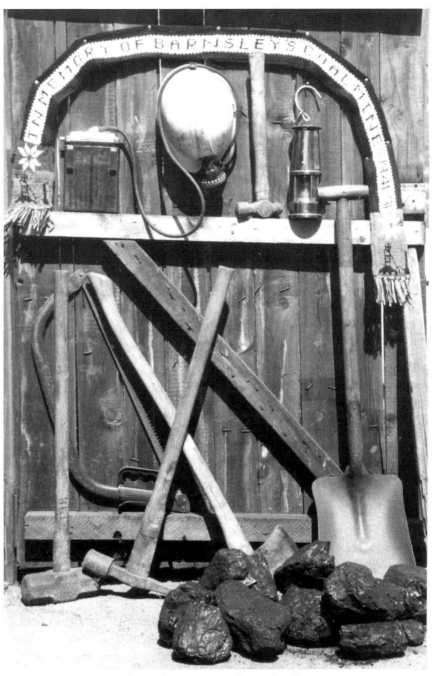

Mining Memorabilia compiled by Stan Potter.

advance/advancing	working the face away from the pit bottom; an exploratory drivage.
aerial flight(s)	system of overhead conveyance of waste material, usually in large suspended buckets, from the pit-head to the **muckstack**.
back ripper/ripping	specialist miner who enlargers underground **roadways** after **advancing**; process of enlarging **roadways** by clearing walls and roof, renewing supports/arches in, for example in 'crush' areas.
back shift	afternoon or night shift.
Baggin	local name for Silverwood Colliery Miners' Institute.
bank	pit-top; the colliery surface near the pit **shaft**.
bannikers	Yorkshire word for short trousers, buckled at the knee, worn by miners.
bar	horizontal roof support of timber or steel usually held in place by posts or **props**.
belt/beltman	miner whose job it is to operate or keep working an underground conveyor belt.
bevin	pay on a **day-wage** basis.
Bevin boy	young person of National Service age selected by lot to work in coal mines during the Second World War. Named after the Labour MP Ernest Bevin, who was Minister of Labour and National Service, 1940–45
big hitter	*slang* name given to a miner who earns high wages, usually via piece work or contract work.
blackclock(s)	beetle or cock-roach (es).
blackleg	a person who works (or takes the place of another person) during a strike, in defiance of a trade union: a strike-breaker.
blacksmith	skilled metalworker working in a pit-top workshop and, occasionally underground; also as a farrier, shoeing ponies.
bob	*slang* for a **shilling** (12 old pence [5 new, decimal pence]).
box hole	underground office near the **pit bottom**.
breech/breeching	a strong leather strap passing round the hindquarters of a shaft-horse; backward movement of a horse.
buddy/buddy system	see butty/butty system.
bummer	*slang* and derogatory name for a person placed in charge; a loafer or idler.
buttonman	miner who drives an underground conveyor **belt**.
butty	a **collier's** helper or friend;cf 'buddy'.
butty system	a practice where middle men [skilled and experienced miners] contract with a mine owner(s) to extract coal, and then engage one or more miners, managing and paying them according to an agreed/shared rates.
cage	a timber or metal compartment of 1–3 decks for hoisting men, **tubs** and materials up and down the **shaft**. Also known as a **chair**.
catch-knocking/lifting	haulage work, handling metal attachments/links to **tubs**, usually in the **pit-bottom**, near the shaft and on/off the **cage**; often undertaken by a young miner.
chain dragging	hauling **tubs** by means of chains.
chair	see **cage**
chargeman/hand	a person with responsibility for a group of other men; often a **beltman**.
check	a numbered aluminium or brass token to prove the presence of a miner in the pit. Also known as a tally. Normally hung in the lamp room. Also see **pay check**.
checkweighman	one of two men responsible for checking the weight of the coal, one appointed by the union, the other by the owner(s).

chock	roof support, originally of interlaced timber, but made of steel and hydraulically [pumped] supported in modern mining, lowered and **advanced** as the conveyor advances.
clip	used in haulage work, a hook-like piece of metal (similar to a pig's tail), placed in a **tub** link and on to a rope.
clogs	hard-wearing shoes worn by miners, leather uppers and wooden soles with replaceable metal strips or studs for gripping surfaces.
coalface	that part of the mine where coal, from a **seam,** is extracted.
collier	a **hewer**, skilled miner who gets (cuts) the coal at the **face**, supports the roof etc.
contractor/contracting	miner employed, as required, by independent person or company, carried out on this basis, moving from job to job/pit to pit.
copper	low-denomination coins such as a farthing, half-penny, penny (and 1–2 p after decimalisation); small change.
corporal	person placed in charge of haulage work and haulage lads; called a 'doggy' in some pits.
crossgate	junction where **roadways** meet.
cundy	Scottish name for the **gob** or **waste** area of a mine.
dataller	a **day-wage** man (as against a piece-rate or contract worker), deployed on a variety of underground labouring jobs eg clearing up falls of rock on haulage roads, workings etc.
day-hole	a shallow pit, usually a **drift mine** or the entrance area, where daylight can be seen or relatively easily reached.
day-wage	a man paid on the basis of shifts worked rather than on piece work eg surface worker, **dataller**, driver, filler.
deputy	a qualified official responsible for underground safety in a mine and the day-to-day deployment of a group of miners. A member of **NACODS**.
deputy's stick	yardstick, similar to a walking stick, used by a **deputy** for measuring **stints**, assisting gas testing etc and a symbolic indication of office.
development work	extension and creation of new and potentially new underground workings; driving **headings** or a new **drift**.
dint/dinting	even/uneven floor/surface areas; repair and maintenance of the same; also deepening floor levels.
dip	angle/slope of rock strata/coal **seam** or **drift**.
district(s)	underground area of mine where particular coal **seam(s)** are located; often a named, identifiable area.
Dosco	company name for a tunnelling, advancing cutter machine.
downcast	**shaft** through which fresh air enters the mine. Also see **upcast**.
draw	upward or downward movement of the **cage**.
drift	entrance tunnel into a mine, driven through rock strata/hillside to reach coal (cf a vertical shaft) or an incline or **heading** made from one part of the underground workings to another, or to the surface.
drift mine	a mine entered by a **drift**.
dudley	portable metal drinking water container of various capacities.
endless rope haulage	haulage mechanism consisting of a long rope or wire driven by an engine round two pulleys by which **tubs** are transported above and below ground.
engineman	man in the engine house responsible for the winding engine or responsible for an underground engine.

face	see **coalface**.
fathom	a measurement of two arms outstretched, six feet (two yards).
filler	miner who loads coal into **tubs** at or by the **coalface**.
fitter	a qualified man who repairs and maintains machinery and equipment underground and on the surface.
flagsheet	sometimes called a **flatsheet**, a metal sheet attached, temporally, from a landing to the **cage** or for use when twisting **tubs** into position.
flatsheet	see **flagsheet**.
gaffer	*slang* for a boss, person in charge.
gantry	a raised and supportive structure on the pit-top, for men, materials or equipment.
gate(s)	an underground **roadway** or tunnel. Also see **crossgate**, **maingate**, **tailgate**; also the gates at the top of the **shaft**, opened and closed during **cage** winding.
gob	area for **waste** /debris, after coal extraction, sometimes called a goaf. Rarely, fires could develop in such areas where coal was left behind the **gob**.
grafter	hard-worker.
gummings/gummer	waste/fine coal after cutting, cleared away by a person with that responsibility.
half a crown	two shillings and six pence (12.5p).
hand-got	coal extracted by traditional 'pick and shovel' methods.
headgear or headstocks	timber (before 1912) or steel frame with pulley wheels suspended over the **shaft**, erected to haul (powered by a steam or electric engine) the **cage**.
heading	a drivage in **advance** of any **coalface** so as to evaluate mining conditions ahead or to reach a **seam** for future production.
hewer	see **collier**.
holing	old name for manually cutting under the **coal seam**.
hopper	metal cone-shaped receptacle.
horsekeeper	person in charge of, and who looks after, the horses/ponies in a mine; also known as **ostler** or **stableman**.
inbye	towards the **coalface** (cf **inbye**).
intake	airway along which fresh air is taken into the workings (cf **return**).
jigger pick	small pneumatic **drill.**
jinny	an incline.
joy loader	**heading** machine.
laik	*dialect* word meaning to play or take time off work.
lamp cabin/room	pit-top building where lamps were housed and issued.
lashing chains	for attaching tubs onto a rope.
level	a drivage tunnel following the course of a **seam** of coal from the surface.
lid	wooden block or wedge.
limmers	shafts which attach the pony to the **tub**.
linesman/lineslad	a surveyor's young assistant.
locker	piece of timber or steel inserted in wheel to stop a **tub** running away; a safety device.

lock-out	a colliery closed by the owner during a dispute, usually to get the miners back to work on his terms.
longwall	system of working coal where several men work along a long **coalface** and where pillars are not used, the roof allowed to cave-in behind the line of supports.
maingate	the main **roadway** leading to (or from) each mining district or **coalface** from the pit-bottom.
manhole	refuge hole made at the side of a **roadway** for the shelter of a person **shot-firing** or for safety from runaway tubs etc; a hiding place for a **deputy** to check on **pony drivers**.
market/marketman	a miner deployed in a variety of jobs, for example, covering for an absent miner.
measure	payment via **piece work** or output.
methane	colourless and odourless gas which forms an explosive mixture when in contact with air.
motty	a small disk or token attached to a **tub** with string and tar which identified the source of the extracted coal.
motty-hanger	boy or young miner who sorts tokens at the surface.
muckstack	spoilheap.
NACODS	National Association of Colliery Overmen & Deputies.
NCB	National Coal Board.
NUM	National Union of Mineworkers.
nipper	*slang* name for a young person or boy miner.
nog end	short wooden wedge.
note/big note	itemised weekly statement of earnings of a group of miners, used prior to a share-out of wages.
onsetter/hooker-on	a man who is responsible for the safe movement and loading/unloading of the **cage** at the bottom of the **shaft**, passing messages to the winder by signals.
ostler	see **horsekeeper.**
outbye	away from the face (cf **inbye**).
outcropping	unofficially getting coal from shallow workings, usually by striking miners and their families.
overman	a senior official, usually a promoted **deputy**, responsible for the day-to-day management of men and materials in part of a mine; just below the status of **under-manager**.
pack	a wall of loose material (stones etc) erected and packed tightly with 'muck' and debris at the centre supporting **roadways** near **faces** and after advancing.
paddy	underground railed system of transport, taking men to their work places; a bus taking miners to work.
pan(s)	metal sections at the conveyors which are moved up the **face** during advancing. See **Panzer**.
Panzer	trade-name for metal conveyor which transfers coal from the **face** to the belt. **See Pan(s)**.
pass-by	passage made near the face so as to allow access to supplies etc.

pay check	numbered metal token exchanged for payment of wages.
picket(s)	person or persons stationed outside or near to their or another place of work during an industrial dispute, with the aim of persuading workers not to enter (ie cross the picket line). Pickets, especially so-called 'flying pickets' and 'mass picketing' came to prominence during the miners' strikes of the 1970s and were an important feature of the 1984/85 miners' strike.
piece tin	Scottish word for a **snap tin**.
piece work	work paid according to output and **price lists**.
pillar(s)	mass of coal left to support the roof after excavation. See **pillar-and-stall**.
pillar-and-stall	a system of mining a **seam** of coal in parallel **stalls** advancing forward, leaving **pillars** of coal, to support the roof.
pit bobby	*slang* term for a person, usually a **deputy**, who inspects and 'polices' any irregular or unsafe practice eg hiding a **prop**.
pit boots	strong heavy work shoes (cf **clogs**).
pit-bottom	area at and near the base of the **shaft**, often a cold part of a mine.
pit-hill	surface of the mine near to the headstocks and the top of the **shaft**.
pit muck	accumulated dust dirt on a miner's clothes and body.
pony driver	young miner in charge of a pony, hauling full and empty **tubs** of coal and materials.
power loading	loading coal directly onto a conveyor.
price lists	before nationalisation coal getting was paid on piece rates, so a man's wage depended on the 'percentage', his output, a 'consideration' for bad conditions, timbering, packing etc; rates were agreed between the colliery company/owner and the miners (ie the union eg Yorkshire Miners Association). The rates were complex but were in place more or less permanently untill re-negotiated. The 'percentage' related to the market price of coal.
prop	vertical roof support, usually timber or steel (cf **bar, chock**).
return airway	course of foul air on way to the **upcast shaft** and out of the pit.
roadway	underground passage/tunnel to reach **coalfaces** and through which ventilation passes (cf **intake, return**).
ring	a steel H-section arch used as a permanent roof support.
ripping/ripper	moving stone, dirt etc (see **back ripping**).
roof-bolting	a modern method of securing roof areas without the use of **props**.
scab	derogatory term for a person who continues to work during a strike.
screens	pit-top area where waste material is separated from the coal and where the coal is graded by mechanical riddles, holed plates etc; and by hand, usually by boys and elderly or partly disabled miners.
seam	a layer, bed or strata of coal, usually given a name relevant to its geological or geographic origin eg *Parkgate seam ; Barnsley Bed* (or more generically as *Thin* or *Thick*) and measured in feet and inches.
shaft	the vertical passage, usually circular, sunk from the surface to reach one or more seams. Also see **upcast** and **downcast**.
shearer	name for a modern coal-cutting machine/loader eg Anderton shearer loader.
shift	period of work, usually 'day', 'afternoon' and 'night'.
shilling	12 old pence (now 5p). Also see **bob**.
shot	explosive charge executed by a **shot-firer**.

shot-firing/firer	the blasting by explosives of stone and coal; a person suitably qualified to carry out this operation safely.
slack/sleck	waste, usually shale stone.
snap/snap tin	a miner's portable meal, usually bread and dripping or jam and contained in a metal tin. Also see **piece tin**.
sprag	a short vertical timber support, usually temporary, placed under coal that has been **undercut**; also a short piece of timber (c.4" x 12" inserted between the spokes of a **tub** wheel to prevent it running away on an incline.
stableman	see **horsekeeper**.
staple shaft	an underground relatively narrow shaft connecting one **seam** to another, often used to transport coal via chutes or **tubs** to an existing transport system.
stall	a marked or designated underground working area for extracting coal. See **pillar and stall**.
stemming	packing material such as clay, placed behind explosives in a shot-hole by a **shot-firer**.
stick	see **deputy's stick**.
stint	a marked yardage along a **coalface** allocated to a miner for working in a **shift**.
tailgate	**roadway** leading to the end of a **longwall face**, usually the **return** airway.
tally	small identification disk or **check**.
tension lad	young miner whose task is to check and maintain the tension of a conveyor **belt**.
tippler	mechanical device used to tip **tubs** of coal onto the **screens**.
trammer	young miner who pushes wheeled **tubs** (or trams) along rails to and from the workings.
trapper	a young person assigned to open and close ventilation doors as and when required.
tub	a small wheeled truck used for carrying coal and materials, about seven hundredweight when full of coal.
UDM	Union of Democratic Miners.
under-manager	a qualified person who could take charge of the mine in the absence of the manager and who may have specialised and/or delegated day-to-day managerial duties.
undercut	a cut made either manually or by machine at the bottom of a **coal seam** as part of the extraction method.
upcast	the ventilation **shaft** that carries the foul/stale air away, assisted by a furnace or fan. Also see **downcast**, **return**.
Vesting Day	1 January 1947, the day that most collieries were nationalised (ie placed under state rather than private ownership), forming the **National Coal Board**.
wage rates	see **price lists**.
waste	another name for **gob** or **goaf**.
weight bumps	movement of roof etc in particular areas due to geological pressure.
winder	man who controls the upward and downward movement of the **cage**.
wireman	an assistant to a qualified electrician.
workings	usually, the **coalfaces** where coal is extracted.

'SNAP TIME'

W.Bennett
994

Index